BREWING Made Easy

Joe Fisher & Dennis Fisher

Illustrated by Randy Mosher

A Storey Publishing Book

STOREY

Storey Communications, Inc.
Schoolhouse Road
Pownal, Vermont 05261

The mission of Storey Communications is to serve our customers
by publishing practical information
that encourages personal independence
in harmony with the environment.

Edited by Elizabeth McHale

Cover design and illustration by Randy Mosher

Text design and production by Cindy McFarland

Production assistance by Robin O'Herin

Indexed by Northwind Editorial Services

Copyright ©1996 by Joe Fisher and Dennis Fisher

Printed in the United States by Vicks Lithograph

10   9   8   7   6   5   4   3   2   1

Library of Congress Cataloging-in-Publication Data

Fisher, Joe, 1966–
    Brewing made easy: from the first batch to creating your own recipes /
    Joe and Dennis Fisher.
    p.   cm.
    "A Storey Publishing Book."
    Includes bibliographical references and index.
    ISBN 0-88266-941-9 (pbk. : alk. paper)
    1. Brewing—Amateurs' manuals. I. Fisher, Dennis, 1963– .   II. Title.

TP570.F535 1996
641.8'73—dc20
                                96-33393
                                    CIP

To Bill and Norma Fulton

Acknowledgments

We would like to thank the American Homebrewers Association and Dena Nishek, editor of *Zymurgy*. Dena has been extremely helpful to us during the development of this book and *Great Beer from Kits*; it was great to work with her on our article "Descending into the Bock Underworld."

Without Ben Gleason's patient guidance, we would not know how to brew. Ben and Don Wagoner helped out a great deal and so did Scott and Bill Nelson of Stout Billy's in Portsmouth, New Hampshire. They are all good friends and fine brewers.

We would like to express our thanks to our editors at Storey Communications, including Elizabeth McHale and Pamela Lappies. Special thanks to Kate Giordano. To our parents, Rose and Jerry Fisher, for their support with this and many other projects, and to Sue Roberts, much thanks.

Contents

Introduction: Why Brew? 1

1. Brewing with Malt Extracts 5

2. Ingredients and Recipe Formulation 23

3. Equipment 41

4. Brewing Tips 47

5. Recipes and Styles 55

Glossary 78

Appendix A: Amounts and Conversions 80

Appendix B: How to Use the Hydrometer 81

Appendix C: Sources 83

Recommended Reading 85

Index 86

Introduction

Why Brew?

Every year tens of thousands of people become home-brewers. It isn't hard to get started. You just walk into your local brewstore and buy an equipment kit, a bag of brewing ingredients, and a book like this one. And then you start to brew. If you like what you made the first time, you brew again. And again.

Suddenly, you *are* a brewer, capable of creating any existing style of beer or of designing your own beers. You start to enter contests, join homebrewing clubs, subscribe to brewing magazines, travel to conventions, and experience the exciting and growing world of beer from the best possible perspective: that of the brewing insider.

The reasons people have for brewing their own beer are many. But for most of us, it comes down to three essential goals: saving money, improving on flavor, and having fun.

Saving Money

This is a great argument for making your own beer. Today an incredible variety of microbrews and imports are available, and there's nothing wrong with that! The fact that this country has finally thrown off the yoke of mediocre commercial beers and embraced the diversity of styles and good taste is cause for celebration. But many of these new beers can be pricey. So why not make beer at home? You can brew simple extract beers such as we describe in this book for just fifty or sixty cents per glass. Compare that with import or brewpub prices! And all-grain brewers can achieve even greater savings.

Improving on Flavor

Most of us who brew at home feel that the taste of our beer is as good as, if not better than, anything on the market. We use the best ingredients and serve our beer perfectly fermented and aged. This is why homebrew is often superior to microbrew. Our beer doesn't have to be shipped anywhere, it doesn't sit on a shelf, and it doesn't have to make a profit. The only people our homebrew has to please are us, our friends, and maybe a panel of judges if we decide to enter it in a contest. We can experiment with the amount and kinds of grain, the type of hops, or the strain of yeast. Ultimately, we can create a recipe that suits our palates perfectly, and it becomes our own *house beer,* something that we will brew again and again in the years to come.

Having Fun

Finally, brewing is fun. There is a deep satisfaction that comes from taking simple ingredients and combining, fermenting, and aging them to produce the age-old and ever-new libation called beer. Some people spend years perfecting just a few recipes; others never brew the same recipe twice. It all depends on what you want to do. Some brewers enjoy complex recipes and elaborate equipment setups; others cultivate simplicity. There is a comfort level of brewing for everybody. You may be satisfied with malt extract brewing and never make the move to all-grain recipes. That's fine with us. We have tried some outstanding extract brews and an equal number of so-so all-grain brews.

Brewing Made Easy is designed for the beginning brewer, and our goal has been to supply accurate information that is easy to understand and apply, so that you can get started in homebrewing the right way. Every brewer does things a little differently, and over time you will undoubtedly develop an individual brewing style that suits you.

We wish you good luck and happy brewing!

1

Brewing with Malt Extracts

Malt extract brewing is the simplest way to make beer, and most people start out this way. Malt extract is the product of grain mashing, in which malt grains are steeped at controlled temperatures to extract the brewing sugars. Then the resulting liquid is reduced until it is a syrup that contains only about 20 percent water.

Mashing is the trickiest stage of brewing, and using malt extracts means that you don't have to mash grain. Later, you can work up to more complex forms of brewing, such as partial mash and all grain. But for now, let's stick to the extracts.

Basic extract brewing is not at all complicated. All you have to do is boil together malt extracts, either in syrup or dry form (often both are used in a recipe), water, and hops. Hops are added to the fermenting brew (wort) at various stages of the boil to provide bitterness, flavor, and aroma. And finally you add yeast after the wort cools.

You can achieve even more simplicity by using can kits, which are cans of hopped malt extract formulated to make a particular beer. The recipe for Redemption Bitter (see page 7), is no more complicated than a simple kit recipe, because it uses malt extract that has already been hopped by the manufacturer.

Brewing at a Glance

1. Sanitize your plastic fermenting bucket, lid, long-handled spoon, fermentation lock, thermometer, plastic tube, and hydrometer in a solution of water and household bleach (use one capful of bleach per gallon of water).

2. Add 1½ gallons of cold water to your fermenting bucket and chill.

3. Immerse the unopened can of malt extract in warm water.

4. Bring 1½ gallons of water to a boil.

5. Add malt extracts to the hot water and boil according to recipe.

6. Turn off heat and add aroma hops.

7. Pour boiled wort into fermenter.

8. Add cold water to make 5 gallons.

9. Take a hydrometer reading.

10. When wort has cooled to 75°F, pitch (add) the yeast.

11. Attach fermentation lock and cover.

12. Ferment 7 to 10 days.

13. Bottle and cap.

The First Recipe

For your first batch of beer, we are going to start off with a simple extract bitter. Bitter is a straightforward pale ale that draws upon the bittering action of hops. It is the standard English pub beer. Easy to brew, bitter is a favorite of ours because it has a lot of character despite its simplicity; and if you really like hops, this is the beer for you.

Redemption Bitter

INITIAL GRAVITY: 1.039–1.045
FINAL GRAVITY: 1.014–1.016

- 3.3 pounds (1.5 kg) Munton & Fison amber hopped malt extract syrup
- 2 pounds (1.4 kg) plain light dry malt extract
- ½ ounce (14 g) East Kent Goldings hop pellets
- 1 or 2 packets Edme ale yeast
- ½ cup (120 ml) corn sugar or ¾ cup (180 ml) dry malt extract for priming

All of these ingredients can be purchased
at any brewstore.

Basic Equipment

You will also need a few pieces of basic equipment.

✔ **Brewpot.** A 16- to 32-quart stainless-steel, enameled-steel, or copper pot is fine for basic extract brewing.

✔ **Long-handled metal or plastic stirring spoon.**

✔ **Plastic fermenting bucket with lid.** A 6.7-gallon plastic fermenter usually comes with the equipment kit.

✔ **Fermentation lock.** A clear plastic airlock allows carbon dioxide to escape during fermentation but keeps air from reaching your beer.

✔ **Hydrometer and plastic hydrometer tube.** The hydrometer is a graduated glass instrument that measures the specific gravity (density) of your wort. You will need the plastic tube (or a glass beaker) to take a sample of your wort for a hydrometer reading.

✔ **Thermometer.** A thermometer, either a floating one (left) or a regular cooking thermometer (right), is useful for telling when it's safe to pitch the yeast. Yeast can stand very cold temperatures, but anything above 90°F will kill it.

✔ **Timer.** A kitchen timer helps you keep track of boiling times. Not essential—but definitely helpful.

Sanitizing

The worst enemy of beer, and the most common cause of first-time-brewing failure, is contamination by microorganisms. The most important thing you can do for your beer is keep your brewing area clean and well sanitized. The standard in commercial breweries is close to operating-room cleanliness. This is necessary because beer-loving bacteria and wild yeast colonies build up wherever beer is present. Always run a rag soaked in sanitizing solution around the brewing area before and after you brew.

You can use a weak solution of unscented household bleach and water, 1 tablespoon bleach per gallon of cold water, to sanitize your brewing equipment. Allow the equipment to soak while you boil the wort. Rinse everything off thoroughly with hot water before using it to remove the chlorine.

Brewing the First Batch

1. **Sanitize** your plastic fermenting bucket, lid, long-handled spoon, fermentation lock, strainer, thermometer, plastic tube, and hydrometer in a weak solution of bleach water (1 tablespoon per gallon). Do this by filling the fermenter with the bleach water solution and soaking the other equipment in it overnight. Rinse *all* equipment *thoroughly* with hot water.

2. **Add** 1½ gallons cold water to the fermenting bucket and chill. Chilling the water helps get the temperature of the beer down to the point where you can pitch the yeast more quickly. Also, it promotes a good **cold break,** which results in a clearer beer.

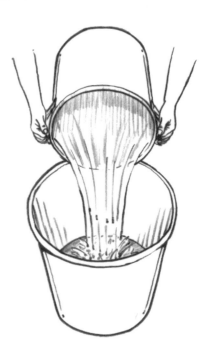

Cold Break

When the hot wort cools, it forms proteins that clump together and eventually either rise to the surface or sink to the bottom. This reaction is called the cold break.

3. **Immerse** the unopened can of malt extract in hot water for about 10 minutes to make it easier to work with.

4. In the brewpot, bring 1½ gallons of water to a boil.

5. **Remove the brewpot from the heat.** Pour the hopped malt extract into the brewpot and scrape any remaining syrup away from the sides of the can. Add the dry malt extract and stir well to dissolve. Return the brewpot to the heat and boil for 20 more minutes.

Full Boil

Eventually, you'll probably want to move on to full boils, where all 5 gallons are boiled for 60 minutes. With full boils, you have greater control over the reactions that take place in the brewkettle.

6. **Remove the brewpot** from the heat when the wort has boiled for 15 minutes, and add East Kent Goldings hop pellets. These will contribute flavor and aroma to the finished beer. Allow to steep for 5 minutes.

7. **Pour** the boiled wort into the fermenter carefully.

Glass Carboys

You may decide to use a glass carboy as your fermenting vessel. If so, let boiled wort cool before you try to pour it into a glass carboy. Sudden temperature changes can cause the glass to crack and/or shatter. See p. 51 for carboy handling tips.

8. **Add enough cold water** to make 5 gallons. (On a standard primary fermenter bucket, the 5-gallon mark is indicated by the thick plastic collar. It is also useful to mark gallon increments on the outside of the bucket with a permanent marker.) Stir thoroughly with the sanitized metal spoon to mix the water with the wort.

9. **Take a sample of the wort** using your sanitized plastic tube. Cool it to 60°F and take a hydrometer reading (see Appendix B: How to Use the Hydrometer). This is your initial *specific gravity*, which should be close to the specified initial gravity listed with the recipe ingredients on page 7.

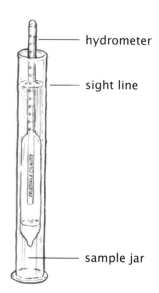

hydrometer

sight line

sample jar

Gravity and Beer

A hydrometer is a graduated instrument used to measure the specific gravity, or density, of beer. By accurately measuring the specific gravity, you can determine (1) when the yeast has finished fermenting, and (2) the amount of alcohol in the beer.

You ordinarily use the hydrometer twice in basic brewing: first to test the specific gravity of the unfermented wort (initial gravity), and second to find the specific gravity of the finished beer (final gravity). The initial reading is taken after the wort has been topped off up to 5 gallons—but before the yeast is pitched—and gives the brewer an idea of the amount of fermentable material in the wort. The second reading is used to confirm that fermentation is complete.

For more information, see Appendix B.

10. **Take the temperature of the wort.** It needs to cool down to 70°F before you can add the yeast. Be sure to rinse the thermometer and shake it down; otherwise it will give you a false reading. Temperatures of 80°F and up are fatal to yeast; temperatures between 60° and 70°F are ideal for ales (a few degrees above or below that range is fine); lower temperatures are necessary for lagers.

Cold-Water Bath

Immersing the fermenter in a cold-water bath can help to bring down the wort temperature quickly.

11. **Add the yeast** and stir it in gently with the sanitized spoon.

12. **Attach the fermenter lid and the fermentation lock.** The fermentation lock must be filled with water. (The gasket in the lid is usually a pretty tight fit for the stem of the airlock. It helps to push against the gasket from the underside of the lid while twisting the airlock.)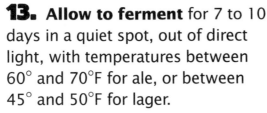

13. **Allow to ferment** for 7 to 10 days in a quiet spot, out of direct light, with temperatures between 60° and 70°F for ale, or between 45° and 50°F for lager.

If your beer is an ale, you should see yeast activity within 24 hours. Bubbles in the fermentation lock will tell you that your wort is fermenting. Eventually, the bubbles will disappear completely. A hydrometer reading for final gravity will tell you if it is safe to bottle at this point — if the specific gravity is within the range specified for final gravity in the recipe ingredients on page 7, then fermentation is complete.

14. **Prime, bottle, and cap the beer** once the fermentation is complete. Priming is a necessary step for carbonation (see page 20). This chore goes a lot faster if you have two people, one to fill the bottles and one to cap. From setup to cleanup, priming and bottling usually takes only an hour or so.

Bottling Equipment

For bottling, you will need the following equipment:

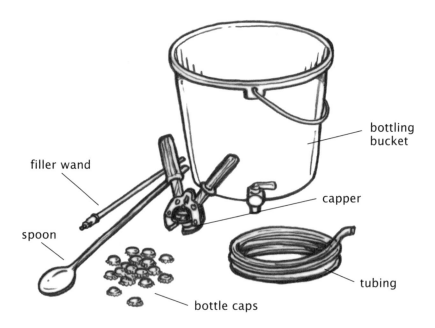

- ✔ **Plastic bottling bucket with spigot.** Equipment kits usually come with a bottling bucket. It can also be used as a secondary fermenter in a two-stage fermentation, which we will talk about in chapter 4.
- ✔ **Plastic tubing.** A short length of ½-inch tubing comes with the equipment kit. You may find that longer tubing is easier to use.
- ✔ **Capper.** The wing capper shown here is a two-levered design.
- ✔ **Bottle caps.** Ordinary crown caps work fine for bottling beer and are readily available at homebrew supply shops.
- ✔ **Long-handled spoon.** Use a metal spoon. It will be the easiest kind to sanitize.

✔ **50 empty long-necked beer bottles.** Use long-necked bottles that require an opener. The bottles should be brown; clear or green ones will admit too much light, giving your beer a skunky aroma.

✔ **Filler wand.** This is a plastic tube with a spring valve at one end. Although it isn't essential, a filler wand certainly comes in handy.

✔ **Saucepans.** You will need these to prepare the priming solution and gelatin, and to sanitize bottle caps.

Ingredients for Priming Beer

✔ **Corn sugar.** Homebrew supply shops carry corn sugar for brewers. The corn sugar is used to prime the beer by giving the yeast an extra bit of food to digest while it is in the bottle.

✔ **Unflavored gelatin** (optional). Gelatin is a fining or clarifying agent. Adding unboiled gelatin to the priming solution removes small particles of protein and yeast residues from the beer.

Bottling Your First Batch

1. **Sanitize the bottles.**
Bottles need to be clean
before they can be
sanitized. If your
bottles have labels,
soaking them a few
extra days will help
you to remove them.
(For more on cleansers,
see page 43.)

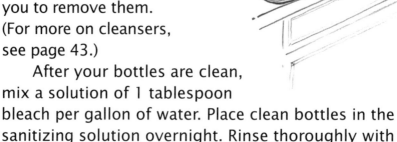

After your bottles are clean,
mix a solution of 1 tablespoon
bleach per gallon of water. Place clean bottles in the
sanitizing solution overnight. Rinse thoroughly with
hot water.

2. **Sanitize the equipment.** Let a plastic bucket,
your plastic tubing (siphon hose), filler wand, and
capper soak in sanitizing solution for at least 30
minutes. Rinse thoroughly with hot water.

If you are using a bottling bucket, sanitize the
spigot and rinse with hot water. Attach the spigot
securely to the bucket.

3. **Sanitize your bottle caps.**
Boil the caps for 5 minutes.

4. **Siphon the fermented beer from the fermenter into the sanitized bottling bucket.**

Place the fermenter higher than the empty, sanitized bucket (see below).

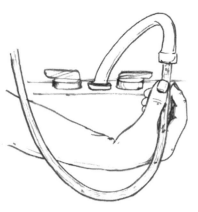

Fill the plastic tubing completely with water, using your thumbs to seal the ends of the tube. Now, holding your thumb over one end, put the other end in the fermenter at the higher level. Hold the free end over an extra container, sink, or drain at alower level, remove your thumb, and allow the water to flow out until the tube is filled with beer. Then, with your thumb over the plastic hose again, hold it over the empty bucket below, and release the beer into the container.

Restart the siphon if it stops flowing. If so, fill the plastic tubing with water again, using your thumb as a seal. Place the other end in the fermenter and allow water to flow out. When beer starts to flow, hold the hose over the lower bucket.

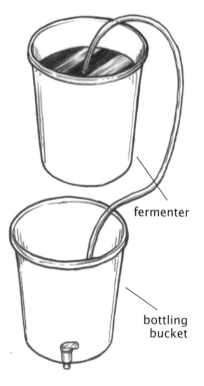

fermenter

bottling bucket

Priming

Before you bottle, you will be "priming" the beer, which simply means adding sugar to the beer. Priming helps to carbonate the beer, by giving the yeast an extra bit of food (the sugar) to digest while it's in the bottle.

The kind of sugar you want to use for priming is dextrose (corn sugar), rather than sucrose (cane sugar). Corn sugar is more readily fermented than is household cane sugar, and not so inclined to produce a "cidery"-tasting beer.

Note: Even corn sugar should not be used in excessive amounts, or the beer will suffer.

5. **Add ¾ cup corn sugar to 2 cups boiling water** to make the priming solution. Stir to dissolve, and remove from heat.

6. **Heat 1 packet of unflavored gelatin in 2 cups water.** Do not boil. Stir to dissolve and add gelatin mixture to priming solution.

7. **Add the priming solution to the beer.** Stir gently with a sanitized spoon.

8. **Move the now-full bottling bucket to a higher position** so that gravity will help the beer to flow. Attach plastic tubing to the bottling bucket spigot. Assemble sanitized filler wand and attach it to the plastic tubing. Open the spigot.

Bottling Alternative

If your equipment kit didn't come with a bottling bucket, you can siphon the beer into bottles. Start the siphon as explained on page 19, and as soon as you draw out beer, crimp the hose and begin filling the bottles.

9. **Fill the bottles.** Press filler wand against the bottom of the bottle to release beer. Lift up to shut off the flow. Leave approximately 1 inch of headspace in your bottles.

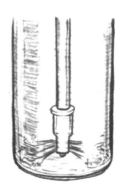

Option: If you aren't using a filler wand, control the flow of beer with your thumb on the plastic tubing.

10. **Cap.** Place a cap on the bottle so it sits evenly. Bring the handles of the capper together, so the jaws meet around the neck of the bottle. Push the handles apart until the cap seats. Now release. The cap will attach, and the weight of the bottle will pull it away from the capper.

Store and Age

Use cardboard case boxes to hold your beer (most homebrew batches will make two cases). Beer stores best in a cool, dark place, such as a cellar. Beers must be aged to allow natural carbonation to take place. Some of the flavors of beer will subtly change with aging. Ales will generally be ready to drink in 2 to 6 weeks. Lagers should be aged for at least 1 to 2 months. Cheers!

2
Ingredients and Recipe Formulation

Now that you have an idea how basic brewing is done, it's time to look at ingredients and to learn a little about how to formulate your own recipes. Brewing ingredients break down into several types. These include malt in some form or other, which provides the fermentable sugars; hops, which provide bitterness, flavor, aroma, and also help preserve the beer; yeast, the tiny organisms that eat the malt sugars and produce alcohol and carbon dioxide (among other compounds); water; and **adjuncts,** which are just about anything else that you add to beer. Adjuncts are a very broad category that includes unmalted grains, non-malt sugars, fruit, brewing herbs other than hops, and spices.

Other brewing ingredients include heading and clarifying agents, which are added to beer to produce a more lasting head of foam and to make a clearer beer, respectively.

Malt Extracts

Concentrated malt extracts are made by commercial malt-sters. Most of the ones you find in homebrew shops are of European origin. There are several different kinds of malt extract available to the homebrewer. All are useful. Which kind you choose for a particular recipe depends on how you want the beer to turn out.

Malt Extract Syrup

Extract syrups come in cans or plastic bags. The syrup is the product of the mashing process, reduced in a vacuum until it contains about 20 percent water and 80 percent soluble solids. The syrup is a thick, molasses-like substance. When adding it to a brewpot, it is a good idea to take the pot off the heat to avoid burning your syrup.

Malt extract syrups come in barley or wheat forms, in light, amber, and dark colors, and may be hopped or unhopped.

Hopped malt extract is just extract syrup to which hops have been added in some form. Usually, hop extracts or oils are used instead of whole hops. The resulting syrup usually has good hop bitterness, but flavoring and aroma hops still need to be added to the recipe.

Lovibond

The color of the malt used in a recipe determines the color of the finished beer. One device for measuring the color of beer is the *Lovibond scale*. The higher the Lovibond number, the darker the malt or beer. The dark grades of crystal malt have a sharp, roasted flavor. Lighter grades have a smooth, rich taste.

Can Kits

Can kits are cans of malt extract that has been blended and hopped to produce a particular style of beer. The kits include a packet of dried yeast under the cap, but it is a good idea to buy fresh yeast, since can kits don't get refrigerated in the brewstores. Can kits are intended to reduce brewing complexity to an absolute minimum. Whatever the supplied directions say, it is always wise to boil the wort for at least 15 minutes and add some aroma hops after the boil. We recommend that you never add corn sugar to these kits; use malt extract instead. Kits often contain corn sugar, which will contribute to a cidery flavor and thin beer. Adding malt extract to a can kit improves flavor and body.

Dry Malt Extract

If the maltster further reduces the amount of water in malt extract syrup, the result is **dry malt extract,** a sticky powder. Except for dry wheat malt extract, dry extracts are all essentially the same except for color. There may be some subtle differences between British and European dry malt extracts, but they're not significant.

Dry malt extract comes in bulk, in extra light, light, amber, and dark. (See chapter 4 for tips on the best way to add dry malt extracts to the boil.)

Malt Grains

Malt grains are sold by the pound in homebrew stores, in bulk or pre-measured in sealed bags. Sometimes they are sold pre-crushed. There are many different kinds available to the homebrewer, each with different characteristics that will contribute unique qualities to your beer.

In the following table of selected malt grains, we provide information as to country of origin, degree Lovibond (a measurement of beer and grain color), description, and recommended amounts of each malt for a 5-gallon batch of beer.

Malt Grain

	Origin	Color	Comments
VIENNA MALT	Germany	4° L	Contributes caramel richness, malty flavor, and amber color. Mostly used in maltier lager styles. Use ¼ pound to 1 pound (110 to 450 g).
MUNICH MALT	Germany	5.7° L	Contributes malty flavor and orange color. Used in Belgian ales as well as dark and light lagers. Use ¼ pound to 1 pound (110 to 450 g).
BISCUIT MALT	Belgium	27° L	Adds a nutty, oatmeal biscuit flavor to beer. Used in milds, brown ales, and Belgian styles. Use ¼ pound to ¾ pound (110 to 340 g).
SPECIAL ROAST MALT	U.S.	45° L	Adds body, roasted malt flavor, and deep orange color. Used in Belgian ales and some lagers. Use ¼ pound to ¾ pound (110 to 340 g).
CRYSTAL MALT	U.S. Germany England	20–90° L	Usually British 2 row, 60° L. Contributes additional sweetness, body, and a golden or reddish color. Used in most styles of beer. Use ¼ pound to 1½ pounds (110 g to 0.7 kg).
CHOCOLATE MALT	U.S. England	400° L	Contributes a nutty, toasted flavor, and brown color. Used in British and Belgian ales, and porters. Use 2 ounces to ¾ pound (57 to 340 g).
ROASTED BARLEY	England	500° L	Dark brown grain made from unmalted barley. Contributes roasted flavor, bitterness, and a brown head. A small amount adds a dark red color. Mainly used in stouts. Use 2 ounces to 1 pound (57 to 450 g).
BLACK PATENT MALT	England	530° L	Roasted malted barley that has had all its flavor driven off. Mostly used for coloring beer. Colors the beer's head and contributes a dry, burnt bitterness unlike that of hops. Used in porters and other black beers. Smoother flavor than roasted barley. Use 2 ounces to ¾ pound.

Adding Grain to Beer

In recipes slightly more advanced than Redemption Bitter (see chapter 1), you will often find a few pounds of malt grains added. Don't worry, it's easy to add them to your wort.

First the malt grains must be crushed. If you haven't bought them pre-crushed, you can crush the grains with a grain mill or a rolling pin (see page 44). Heat 1½ gallons of water to about 150°F. (We use a 2-gallon stainless-steel pot.) Add the grains and steep for 15 minutes. (Do not boil the grains.) The grains will swell up in the pot. In a separate saucepan, boil 2 quarts of water for rinsing.

Now strain the steeping water into your brewpot. Pour some of the rinsing water into the strainer and press down on the grains with your spoon to extract the liquid from the malt. Now you can add your malt extracts to the strained liquid and proceed with your brewing.

Grain Bags and How to Use Them

Grain bags are mesh bags used to contain grains while steeping, somewhat like a giant tea bag. This makes it easier to handle the grains, and allows you to use just one pot for

Grain bags make it easier to add grains to the brewpot.

the operation. To use a grain bag, pour the malt grains into the bag and tie off the neck. Heat 1½ gallons of cold water to about 150°F (66°C). Put the grain bag in the water and let it steep for 15 minutes. Then gently squeeze out the grain bag with your brewing spoon and remove it from the pot. The grain bag can then be placed in a strainer and sparged (or rinsed) with boiled water.

Allow the grain bag to steep for 15 minutes.

Use your spoon to gently squeeze out the grain bag as you remove it.

Hops

Hops are the flowers of the female vine of *Humulus lupulus*. They are available loose, in plugs, and pelletized. (Hops are also available in the form of hop extracts and oils, but we won't be using them here.) Loose hops are whole hop flowers that come in 1- or 4-ounce bags. Hop plugs are whole hops that have been compressed into ½-ounce cakes that will loosen up in the boil. Pelletized hops have been ground and pressed into pellets. These are available in 1-ounce

hop plug   loose hops   pelletized hops

pouches. They take up less space per ounce than loose or plug hops, but they are also more difficult to remove from the wort.

Bittering hops, used to add bitterness to the finished beer, are usually added early in the boil. Through the duration of the boil, the essential oils that provide flavoring and aroma are boiled off while the alpha acids undergo a process of isomerization (chemical transformation) that releases their bittering potential.

Flavoring hops are added during the later part of the boil. Some types of beers may use two or even three different varieties of flavoring hops. Aromatic or finishing hops are added immediately after the final boil and provide a delicately hoppy "nose" (that is, aroma). Adding hops during the secondary fermentation, known as dry hopping, can also impart a fresh hop aroma to the beer.

Hop Varieties

Different hops have different uses. Some are predominantly bittering, flavoring, or finishing hops, and some fulfill a combination of functions, depending on when and in what amount they are added to the wort.

Alpha Acids

Alpha acids are the acids that form the main bittering agents in hops. The potential bitterness of hops is expressed in *alpha acid units (AAU),* which is calculated as the percentage of alpha acids in the hops x the weight of the hops.

Low bitterness	= 2 to 4% alpha acid content
Medium bitterness	= 5 to 7% alpha acid content
High bitterness	= 8 to 12% alpha acid content

INGREDIENTS AND RECIPE FORMULATION

Hop Varieties

Name	Percentage Alpha Acids	Origin	Description and Uses
CASCADE	5–7%	U.S. Canada	Spicy floral aroma. Signature hop of American pale ales. Bittering, flavoring, aroma, dry hopping.
EAST KENT GOLDINGS	5–7%	England	Classic British ale hop. Delicate, subtly spicy hop. Bittering, flavoring, aroma, dry hopping.
EROICA	10–13%	U.S.	Very bitter; some aromatic qualities. Often used to bitter darker British ales.
FUGGLES	4–7%	England U.S.	Traditional British ale hop. Mild, earthy. Bittering, flavoring, aroma, dryhopping.
HALLERTAU	4–6%	Germany	Traditional lager hop. Clean and floral. Bittering, flavoring, aroma.
NORTHERN BREWER	7.5–9.5%	Germany U.S. Belgium	Bold, bitter, aromatic. Brewer aroma.
SAAZ	4–6%	Czech Republic	Traditional pilsner hop. Floral, elegant. Bittering, flavoring, aroma, dry hopping.
STYRIAN GOLDINGS	5–7.5%	Slovenia	Excellent ale hop. Aromatic, clean. Bittering, flavoring, aroma, dry hopping.
TETTNANG	4–6%	Germany	German and American lager hop. Spicy and distinctive. Bittering, flavoring, aroma.
WILLAMETTE	5–7.5%	U.S.	Aromatic, developed as a slightly spicier American Fuggles. Bittering, flavoring, aroma, dry hopping.

The alpha acids give you an idea of the bitterness potential of each hop, with higher alpha values indicating greater bitterness.

Yeast

Once all the necessary chemical reactions have taken place in the different stages of the boil, the wort is chilled and the critical component of yeast takes over to complete the transformation from ingredients to beer. Brewing yeast comes in two basic types: top-fermenting ale yeast and bottom-fermenting lager yeast.

Top-Fermenting and Bottom-Fermenting Yeasts

Top-fermenting yeasts are so called because they accumulate at the top of the fermenter. They favor warm temperatures, act rapidly, and tend to produce esters and other organic compounds that provide a variety of flavors to beer. The use of top-fermenting yeast in ales accounts for their highly complex flavors.

Bottom-fermenting yeasts accumulate at the bottom of the fermenter. They act at lower temperatures than ale yeasts, and over a much longer period of time. This tends to produce a beer with more subtle flavor and little or no yeasty character.

Yeast is available as **dried yeast, liquid yeast,** and **liquid yeast packs.** Whatever form it's in, you need to keep it refrigerated until just before you're ready to brew.

Dried yeast comes in a packet just like bread yeast and is very easy to use. Unlike liquid yeast, it takes off rapidly (within a few hours) and finishes rapidly; there isn't a lot of waiting around. It can also be hydrated for slightly faster results: Dissolve the yeast in a sanitized cup with ½ cup of warm (70° to 80°F) water and allow to sit for 10 to 15 minutes before pitching (adding yeast to wort).

Liquid yeast comes in a vial and can be used just as easily. Warm to room temperature and shake it up before pitching.

Liquid yeast packs (for example, Wyeast) contain a liquid yeast culture that is kept separate from a malt extract food source in a plastic bag. To use the yeast, you have to break the plastic bag inside the envelope, being careful not to break the envelope.

To break the bag, place the pack on a flat surface and give it a good whack with your hand. Wyeast packs have to work for 3 to 7 days (older packs have to work longer) before you can add it to wort. Leave the pack undisturbed in a warm place. The yeast will begin to eat the malt extract in the pack, producing carbon dioxide, which will eventually cause the pack to swell up like a balloon.

When ready to pitch, cut off one corner of the pack with a pair of sanitized scissors.

Finings

Finings are clarifying agents added to the wort during the boil or fermentation. They precipitate out proteins, yeast, and other solids from the wort, resulting in a clearer finished beer. The most commonly used finings are Irish moss and gelatin.

Yeast Varieties

Description*

DRIED ALE YEAST

Edme Ale Yeast — A fast-acting yeast with some fruity esters. (65–70°F)

Munton & Fison Muntona Ale Yeast — Fast-acting yeast with some fruity esters. (65–70°F)

Nottingham Ale Yeast — Fast-acting, nutty-tasting yeast. Produces a dry, crispale. (65–70°F)

Whitbread Ale Yeast — Very reliable, fast-starting yeast blend. Has a unique flavor. Only ale yeast capable of cool-temperature fermentation. (65–70°F)

Windsor Ale Yeast — Fast acting, with only moderate attenuation. Leaves full body. Good for stouts, porters, bitters. (65–70°F)

DRIED LAGER YEAST

Yeastlab Amsterdam Lager — A good all-purpose lager yeast that creates a clean, crisp taste. (58–68°F)

LIQUID ALE YEAST

Wyeast #1968 London Ale — Bold, woody, slight diacetyl (butterscotch) touch. Recommended for most British ales. (64–70°F)

Wyeast #3068 Weihenstephan Wheat — Very reliable, clovelike. For Bavarian wheat beer. (68°F)

Yeastlab A08 Trappist Ale — Fruity, phenolic, alcohol-tolerant yeast. (64–70°F)

Yeastlab A05 Irish Ale — Mildly acidic with diacetyl note. Recommended for use in stouts and porters. (65–68°F)

Yeastlab W51 Bavarian Weizen — Spicy, phenolic, clovelike. Produces classic Bavarian wheat beers. (66–70°F)

LIQUID LAGER YEAST

Wyeast #2112 California Lager — Warm-fermenting lager yeast, prefers temperatures around 60°F. Recommended for use in California Common beers. (60°F)

Yeastlab L32 Bavarian Lager — Rich, malty, and sweet. Recommended for bocks, Vienna lagers, maerzens, & Oktoberfests. (48–52°F)

Yeastlab L34 St. Louis Lager — Clean, crisp, and fruity. High attenuation, medium flocculation. Recommended for American-style pilsners. (50–52°F)

Yeastlab L35 California Lager — Malty, woody, with some fruitiness. Recommended for California Common beers. (64–66°F)

*Temperature ranges given are for optimal fermentation.

INGREDIENTS AND RECIPE FORMULATION

Irish Moss

Irish moss is a dried, pulverized seaweed that is added during the boil to help coagulate proteins. It is much more effective if hydrated (soaked) overnight before brewing. Most of our recipes call for 1 teaspoon in 1 cup warm water. It's a good idea to add Irish moss to the boil, whether the recipe calls for it or not—unless you're brewing a Weizen or a Wit beer.

Gelatin

Plain, unflavored gelatin is added during secondary fermentation or at bottling as a fining agent. One packet of gelatin added to 1 pint of water is sufficient for 5 gallons of beer. You can make up this mixture at the same time that you boil your bottle caps and priming sugar. But don't boil the gelatin, or it will become useless. Gelatin produces very clear beer, and even makes pouring the beer easier, because it coagulates the sediments at the bottom of the bottle.

Recipe Formulation

Once you have been brewing for a while, you will probably want to start creating your own recipes. This is one of the most rewarding aspects of homebrewing, and is not as difficult as it might sound. As you follow the recipes in this book, you will soon get a feel for what characteristics different ingredients add to the finished product. You will develop preferences not only among beer styles, but also among types of hops, yeast, and malt extracts.

Choosing a Style

There is no end to the styles of beer you can brew, or the variations within each style. If you like a microbrewed or imported brew, why not try to replicate it in your own home brewery? You can also take advantage of the hundreds of different kinds of can kits available and experiment with modifying them according to certain beer styles.

Basing a recipe on a can kit is one way for beginning brewers to approach beer styles. Another method is to try and match your recipe to a style description. We've included a chart showing target specific gravity, Alpha Acid Units, comments, and amounts of flavoring hops for each style (see page 40). If you know the basic parameters for a style and the ingredients that go into it, there's no reason that you can't create recipes for that style.

Selecting Malts and Extracts

There are three things to consider when choosing malt extracts: **specific gravity, color,** and whether to use a **hopped or unhopped extract.** Specific gravity will tell you certain things about the finished beer, such as how much alcohol it will have and how malty it will be. Choosing a light, amber, or dark malt will determine what color the beer will be. Unless we're brewing a very basic beer, we like to use malt grains to color our beer (more on that shortly). If you use hopped malt extract (or even a can kit) in your recipe, you'll need to use less hops. If you use an unhopped extract, you'll need more hops, and you'll have to boil them longer.

The style chart (page 40) will tell you roughly what the specific gravity of each style should be. A general rule of

This Amazing Wheel of Beer (a kind of wort slide rule developed by Randy Mosher) helps you calculate what each ingredient contributes to your beer. The wheel is available in most homebrew supply shops.

thumb is that 1 pound of malt extract syrup will yield about 6 to 7 points of specific initial gravity. One pound of dry malt extract will give you about 8 to 9 points of specific initial gravity. (A point of specific gravity is equal to .001 added to the specific gravity of water, which is 1.000; thus, 1 pound of malt extract syrup will yield a specific initial gravity of about 1.006 to 1.007.) However, calculating specific gravity is an exact science, and if you want to know precisely what each ingredient contributes to your beer, tools such as the Amazing Wheel of Beer can help.

Almost all beer styles benefit from the addition of malt grains. Grains contribute many subtle characteristics that are missing from malt extract alone. The amount and type used will depend on the characteristics you are trying to extract from the grain. In the case of very dark beers such as stout, ⅛ to ½ pound of black patent malt will give your beer better color than will dark malt extract alone. A mix of Belgian malts or different crystal malts can lend the beer a rainbow of colors from amber to garnet. Crystal malt will add sweetness and depth to the body of a beer, while pale malt can lend a fresh grain flavor that is often lacking in extracts. The list of grains on page 26 gives suggestions for amounts and styles.

Selecting Hops

The first thing to consider when choosing hops is bitterness. The second is the characteristics contributed by the hop variety you've chosen, and whether that character is suitable for the style of beer you want to brew. Once you've determined these things, picking the hops should be a simple matter of deciding which varieties to use.

In the style chart (see page 40), we use Alpha Acid Units (AAUs) to describe bitterness. AAU is a measure of the bitterness potential of hops for a given volume of beer. AAU is determined by multiplying the percentage of alpha acids in a given hop variety by the number of ounces used. For instance, 2 ounces of Cascade hops (5 to 7 percent alpha acid) would give 10 to 14 AAU: (5 to 7) x 2 = (10 to 14). Match the AAU given in the style chart to the AAU value of the hops you plan to use.

Flavoring is a bit less scientific. We've given rough estimates for flavoring hops in the style chart. One of the factors that distinguishes recipes and styles from each other is the variety and amounts of flavoring hops they use, as well as the time they spend in the boil. This is an area where homebrewers experiment according to their individual tastes. Hoppy styles such as India Pale Ale (IPA) could easily take more flavor or bitterness than we've indicated. Consult the Hop Varieties chart (page 30) for suggestions on which hops to use in different beer styles.

Aroma and dry hops are another area that shouldn't be overlooked when designing beer recipes. We make suggestions about the amount of aromatic and dry hops to use, but it's really up to you, the individual homebrewer. The freshest and most aromatic hops you can find are the best for aroma and dry hopping. Remember that a large part of your sense of taste is actually that of smell; so good beer aroma equals better beer taste.

Selecting Yeast

Usually, the first decision you will make is whether to brew a lager or an ale. That will determine what type of yeasts you will choose from. The next step is to choose between dry and liquid yeast. Most beginning homebrewers use dry yeast, although liquid yeast that is started correctly will generally start fermenting faster.

Once you graduate to more advanced brewing, you'll want to take advantage of the many varieties of liquid yeast. If you want to brew Belgian, London, English, Irish, American, or Canadian ales, specific liquid yeasts are available. So are Danish, Munich, Pilsner, American, Bavarian, and St. Louis lager yeasts. Depending on what style of beer you want to brew, the choices can be many. Some styles of beer, however, such as Weizen and California Common, make more exacting demands for specific yeast characteristics, limiting the number of choices.

Adjusting Water Chemistry

The best water for homebrewing is pure and relatively free of chemicals such as chlorine. If your tapwater tastes good and smells good, then it is probably fine to use for extract brewing. It's really only when you get into all-grain brewing that water quality becomes crucial.

As a general rule, British ales are brewed using hard water, and European lagers are brewed with soft water. If your water is soft, it's easy to harden it using Burton water salts or gypsum. They are available at your homebrew store. Between 1 and 2 teaspoons added to the brewing water before the grains are steeped should be enough. If your water is already hard it will be fine for brewing ales, but you might want to track down a supply of soft water before you try to brew authentic lagers.

Many bottled waters are less suitable for brewing than is tap water because some minerals essential for brewing have been distilled or filtered out. If you are concerned about water quality, filtering your water with a simple charcoal filter is your best bet.

Recipe Design: A Crash Course

The best way to teach recipe design is to show you how we do it. We'll start with Belgian Tripel, a malty, strong ale.

Consulting the style chart, we find that the target initial gravity should be between 1.065 and 1.089, or roughly 9 pounds of fermentables (ingredients containing sugar to be fermented). In our Belgian Tripel we use honey, so we'll add 3 pounds of honey to 6.6 pounds Northwest gold extract syrup. (Any brand of malt extract would do—Northwest is a favorite because it's fairly inexpensive and of generally good quality.)

Now we'll pick malt grains. We note from the chart on page 26 that Vienna malt and Munich malt add interesting characters and aren't too dark for Tripel. We'll add ½ pound of each. Looking at the chart again, Tripel has 5 to 7 AAUs. Adding 1 ounce of Styrian Goldings hops will give exactly the right bitterness (5 to 7 percent alpha acids x 1 ounce = 5 to 7 AAU). We'll add ½ ounce of Saaz hops for dry hopping.

Estimating Fermentables

A simple formula, based on the target specific initial gravity, can be used to estimate the amount (in pounds) of fermentables you need to include in your recipe: Divide the last 2 digits of the initial gravity by 10.

In the case of our Tripel, 89 ÷ 10 = 8.9 pounds of fermentables.

That leaves the yeast. Belgian ale yeast doesn't come dried, but both Wyeast and Yeastlab offer it in liquid form. Belgian yeasts are, however, wildly variant and you may want to seek out more yeasts and repeat batches with different strains.

Style Guidelines for Recipe Formulation

STYLE	INITIAL GRAVITY	AAU	COMMENTS	FLAVORING HOPS
Alt	1.040–1.057	12–22	Store cold.	no
Barleywine	1.090–1.110	50–60	English hops	3 oz.
Bitter	1.030–1.038	7–10	½ oz. aroma	1–2 oz.
Bock	1.064–1.074	12–20	no aroma	½–1 oz.
Brown Ale	1.040–1.055	8–12	½ oz. aroma	1–2 oz.
California Common	1.047–1.052	12–15	Ferment warm, dry hop.	½ oz.
Cream Ale	1.042–1.048	7–9	Store cold.	no
Czech Pilsner	1.045–1.052	10–14	½ oz. aroma	½–1 oz.
Dubbel	1.040–1.080	7–8	½ oz. aroma	1 oz.
Dunkel	1.045–1.058	12–15	¼ oz. aroma	1–2 oz.
ESB	1.046–1.060	9–11	½–1 oz. aroma	H–2 oz.
German Pilsner	1.040–1.050	12–16	½ oz. aroma	½–2 oz.
India Pale	1.050–1.070	14–18	1 oz. dry hop	1–2 oz.
Maerzen	1.050–1.065	12–15	½ oz. aroma	½–2 oz.
Mild	1.030–1.040	6–8	½–2 oz. aroma	no
Old	1.052–1.080	15–17	½ oz. aroma	no
Pale Ale	1.042–1.060	12–14	1 oz. dry hop	1–2 oz.
Porter	1.040–1.060	9–11	½–1 oz. aroma	no
Scotch Ale	1.040–1.050	7–8	Low carbonation	no
Stout, Dry	1.035–1.050	12–15	roasted barley	no
Stout, Sweet	1.035–1.060	9–12	Add lactose.	no
Tripel	1.065–1.089	5–7	½ oz. dry hop	1 oz.
Weizen	1.040–1.055	4–6	40–60% wheat malt	no

3

Equipment

Here we've included equipment and brewing materials that we didn't get a chance to talk about in chapter 1. The topic of brewing equipment is huge, and collecting brewing equipment is one of the joys of homebrewing. Some people carry this to an extreme and end up building what amount to home microbreweries, jammed with interesting technology. (Serious gadgeteers should check out *Brew Ware* by Karl F. Lutzen and Mark Stevens for suggestions.) Though you don't need all of that stuff just to make good beer, the equipment below is all highly useful to the serious brewer.

✔ **Airlock or fermentation lock.** There are several kinds of airlocks available. We recommend the two-piece fermentation lock (at left) because it is simple and easy-to-clean. Assemble the fermentation lock and fill halfway to the top with tap water. With the plastic lid in place, the two small holes will allow CO_2 to escape.

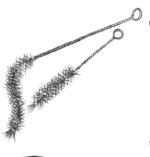

✔ **Bottle brush and carboy brush.**
These are used for cleaning bottles and scrubbing out the top of the carboy.

✔ **Bottle washer.** This is a U-shaped brass valve that screws into a faucet. The end of the valve points up, so you can invert the bottle or carboy and stick it over the top. These generally sell for less than $15 and the savings in hot water alone makes them worth the price. You can buy a separate adapter that will fit any faucet.

✔ **Carboy.** This is a large, transparent glass bottle used as a fermenter. To sanitize the carboy, fill it up to the top with sanitizing solution and leave it overnight.

NOTE: Avoid pouring hot wort into a cold, empty carboy or it might crack. Always pour a gallon of cold water into the bottom of the carboy before adding wort.

✔ **Cleansers and sanitizers.** All equipment must be clean before it can be sanitized. The following are just some of the options you have for cleansers and sanitizers.

> **Baking soda.** Sodium bicarbonate is a nontoxic abrasive cleanser (not a sanitizer) that can be used to clean beer equipment such as carboys and brewpots.
>
> **B-Brite.** Hydrogen peroxide–based cleanser (not a sanitizer). Excellent for removing stubborn beer deposits on equipment. Mix 1 tablespoon per gallon of warm water.
>
> **Household bleach.** Unscented household chlorine bleach is a great sanitizing product for use in brewing, because it is easy to handle, cheap, and safe. Mix 1 tablespoon per gallon of water for sanitizing bottles and equipment. Always use cold water in the solution, since heat destroys the sanitizing properties of bleach. It is necessary to rinse the bottles thoroughly with hot water.
>
> **Iodophor.** Iodine-based sanitizer. Effective sanitizer for all types of brewing equipment. Unlikely to produce any off flavors. Requires no rinsing when diluted to correct concentration.

 ✔ **Funnel.** A large plastic funnel is very useful when you start fermenting in a carboy.

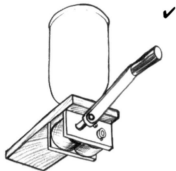

✔ **Grain mill.** Most homebrew stores will have an electric grain mill, so you can have the grain crushed there. Home mills such as the Philmill are also available.

Philmill

Option

Small amounts of grains can be crushed with a rolling pin. Put them inside a plastic freezer bag, lay the bag on a flat surface, and use a rolling pin or can to crack the grains.

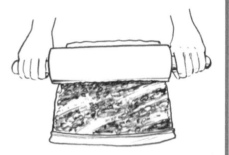

Hop bag

✔ **Hop bag.** Similar to a grain bag (see chapter 2). Used for confining dry hops in the secondary fermenter.

✔ **Kettles.** Enamelware canners or stainless-steel pots can be used as boiling kettles. Avoid plain steel and iron—they can give your beer a metallic taste.

✔ **Notebook.** A beer notebook is a valuable resource. Use it to keep track of when you brewed, what ingredients you used, how long you boiled, how long the beer took to ferment, any problems you encountered, when you bottled, and how you liked the beer. Writing down your observations and procedures will allow you to reproduce any beers you especially liked (or avoid problems) in the future.

A 10-pound spring scale is useful for weighing malt.

✔ **Scale.** Scales are useful for weighing malt grains, hops, and adjuncts.

An ounce scale comes in handy for measuring hops and adjuncts.

✔ **Stopper.** You should have two rubber stoppers for your carboy: one with a hole in it to allow for the blow-by tube and fermentation lock, and a solid one for those times when you need to stop the neck of the carboy. Plastic carboy caps are also inexpensive, easy to use, and durable.

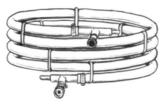

✔ **Strainer.** A metal strainer is useful for rinsing grains and straining spent hops from wort. It should fit inside your funnel.

✔ **Wort chiller.** This device is used to cool wort before pitching the yeast.

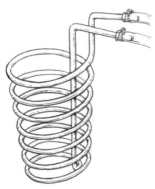

The immersion wort chiller consists of a coil of copper tubing attached to the cold-water tap and immersed in the wort (it must be sterilized first).

Counterflow wort chillers have two coils, one inside the other. Hot wort flows through the inner coil and cold water flows around it in the outer coil.

Immersion wort chiller

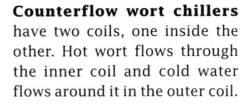

Counterflow wort chiller

4
Brewing Tips

Homebrewers collect not just brewing equipment, but also useful tips and techniques. Some brewers hoard their secrets, but most are happy to share what they know. Good places to pick up new ideas on how to make your brewing procedures simpler, more sanitary, or otherwise better are your local homebrew store, meetings of your homebrew club, and in brewing books and magazines. Homebrewing is not an exact science. Every brewer has a preferred, unique way of doing things — his own particular style.

In this chapter, we'll talk about a few more advanced brewing topics as well as some handy practices that have come our way in the course of our own brewing. It's not a bad idea to write down your own proven strategies in your brewing notebook, so that you won't forget them next time.

Adding Dry Malt Extract

The easiest way to add dry malt extract to a recipe using grains is to put the extract into your second brewpot and strain the sweet wort from the first brewpot into it. Stir to dissolve, then add your extract syrup.

Wort-Cooling Alternative

Recycled 2-liter plastic soda bottles make an economical alternative to wort chillers. Fill several with tap water and put them in the freezer. When you want to cool wort, take them out of the freezer and quickly sanitize them (refrigerators and freezers are breeding grounds for bacteria) and drop them carefully in the brewpot or fermenter to cool off wort quickly.

Primary and Secondary Fermentation

Primary fermentation is the first, explosive phase of fermentation, usually taking just a few days, and secondary fermentation is a more sedate stage that can take weeks.

The point of secondary fermentation is to move beer to a second vessel to get it off the spent yeast, settled proteins, and other decaying matter that have settled in the wort. Therefore, using a secondary fermenter (especially a glass one) can really help improve the clarity and flavor of beer. "Racking" the beer simply means to transfer it by siphoning to a sanitized secondary fermenter, either the one provided with your equipment set or a glass carboy.

Racking setup

The Blow-by System

The blow-by system is a standard homebrewing technique, important during the primary fermentation, when the beer produces a huge foamy head, or **kraeusen.** In the bucket-type primary fermenter, the kraeusen cannot escape and eventually sinks back into the beer. This can contribute off flavors to the homebrew. The only way to get rid of it is to open the fermenter and scoop up the brownish foam with a sanitized spoon, but this can allow microorganisms a chance to get at your beer and spoil it.

The blow-by gets around this problem by allowing much of the kraeusen to escape the fermenter through the plastic tube. Be sure to use a large tube, 1 or 1½ inches in diameter or as large as the inner diameter of the opening in the carboy will allow.

To put together a blow-by setup, you will need:

✔ 5½-gallon glass carboy
✔ 3-foot length of 1- or 1½-inch plastic tubing
✔ Clean milk jug half full of water

To use the blow-by system, put the wort in the carboy and pitch the yeast. Set the carboy and jug on a large, flat receptacle such as a jelly-roll pan. Fit the sanitized plastic tube into the the neck of the carboy. Put the free end of the tube into the milk jug. The whole thing forms an airlock.

Once primary fermentation is complete, remove the blow-by and substitute the airlock and stopper in the carboy.

Is It Beer Yet?

The airlock or fermentation lock can be used to tell if the beer is finished. If bubbles have stopped coming out of the airlock, or if they only appear once every 90 seconds or longer, then the beer is ready to bottle.

Carboy Jackets

Because carboys are clear, it is important to cover them with something to keep out light during fermentation. Exposure to light will cause the hops in beer to become "lightstruck," and give them a skunky flavor. This is why most beers come in dark-colored bottles.

A dark plastic trash bag with a hole in the bottom for the airlock will make an adequate carboy cover. In our home brewery, we use some old army jackets. We just drape the jackets over the carboys and zip up the fronts. This provides plenty of darkness, as well as a measure of protection for the glass bottles.

Carboy Tip

If you have room, store carboys in a closet or cellar; that's the simplest way to keep carboys out of sunlight.

Emptying a Carboy

One of the trickiest jobs in brewing is emptying a carboy. A full carboy is heavy and fragile, and if it is wet it can really be a handful. As you pour, air is forced into the narrow neck of the bottle and water is forced out, and the carboy will glug and splash water all over the place. To avoid this problem, take a racking tube, which is a long, rigid plastic tube used in siphoning, and place it in the carboy. Be sure to keep the end of the tube in the air bubble that forms as you pour. This will allow air to flow easily into the bottle, avoiding a potential mess.

Cleaning the Carboy

Once you've racked your beer into bottles, you will be faced with the task of cleaning your carboy. Fermentation leaves a thick sludge of spent yeast in the bottom of the fermenter. Pouring a gallon or so of warm water into the carboy and sloshing it around will help get rid of this. There will also be a ring of beer residue around the neck of the bottle. This can be scrubbed off with a bent bottle brush. Finally, invert the carboy over your bottle washer and blast out any remaining gunk. If your carboy is very dirty, fill it with a bleach solution or a solution of baking soda and water and allow it to soak for a few days.

Carboy-Handling Tips

You will want to handle your carboy carefully. Easy-to-attach carboy "handles" are available through home-brew supply outlets, and they cost only a few dollars. **Note:** Use handles on empty carboys only.

Keep your glass carboy in a plastic milk crate for easier handling when it is full.

About Lagers

In this basic brewing book, we've tended to concentrate on ales because they are quick and easy to brew. Lagers are a little more complex. Lager yeasts are a different strain from ale yeasts and accumulate on the bottom of the fermenting vessel, rather than on top as with ales. Therefore, lagers are called "bottom-fermenting" beers, and ales are "top fermenting." Lagers require cooler temperatures than do ales, usually in the 40° to 50°F range rather than the 60° to 70°F environment suitable for ales. For this reason, it's best to brew your lagers in fall or winter.

Lagers also require a secondary fermentation in a separate vessel. After primary fermentation is complete, and the bubbles in the airlock have slowed to once every few seconds, the beer is racked off into the secondary fermenter, usually a carboy. It is then left in a cold place to "lager" for several months. The resulting beer is very clear and clean tasting. Malt characteristics are quite evident in lagers.

Bottles

Bottles are available cheaply from bottle redemption and distribution centers, or you can collect your own. Your homebrew store may have inexpensive used bottles as well as new ones. We like to use 28-ounce (820-ml) glass soda bottles that we get from a local bottling works and we recycle any 22-ounce microbrew bottles and swing-type Grolsch bottles that come our way. These bottles don't require caps and can be used many times before the gasket on the stopper will need replacement.

Beer Labels

Labels can make a spiffy presentation for your beer. You can buy them in the homebrew store, or just make them up yourself. If you have a computer with a graphic design program, it will be easy to make your own labels. Cut them to size and stick them to the bottles with a little glue.

Beer Glasses

Gone are the days when you had to serve your beer in a water tumbler or football mug. Most homebrew stores now stock a variety of interesting beer glasses and steins. Glass factory outlets are also a good place to look for drinking accessories. Our favorite everyday beer drinking glasses are 16-ounce English-style pub glasses. These are heavy, thick-walled tumblers that will stand up to a lot of use.

Serving Tips

Whatever you choose to drink from, you should make sure it is rinsed really well after washing. Waxes in dish detergents will rapidly deflate the head on beer.

Beer may be served in glasses that are chilled, but they shouldn't be extremely cold.

Serving Homebrew

Remove the cap with a bottle opener and pour the beer all at once without setting it down. Pour slowly, tilting the glass to avoid building up too much of a foamy head, and then level the glass for the last ½ inch. Stop pouring when the sediment starts moving toward the neck of the glass. With a little practice you will be able to pour out most of the beer, leaving the sludgy sediment behind.

Beer I.D.

A simpler way to identify beer is just to write the beer name initials and date on plain bottle caps with a magic marker: For instance, Monitor Dopplebock brewed on June 19, 2001, would be written "M.D. 6-19-01." Then you can note what beer the initials refer to on a list tacked up on a wall in your beer cellar.

5

Recipes and Styles

The following recipes are a selection of the many we have developed in our years of homebrewing. They've all been formulated to be easy to brew and tasty to drink. In most cases we've included a very simple and then a slightly more complicated version of each beer, so that you can get a feel for the style before attempting something a little more challenging.

We encourage you to experiment with these recipes. Adding a little more grain, or a different strain of hops, can have a significant effect on the flavor, color, and aroma of the finished beer. Many homebrewers use an experimental approach to brewing, changing the recipes slightly each time they brew, and letting their taste buds guide them.

California Common

California Common is one of our native American beers—a smooth, well-hopped beverage brewed from lager yeasts at ale temperatures.

Demologos Common Beer

INITIAL GRAVITY: 1.044–1.049
FINAL GRAVITY: 1.011–1.016

4 pounds (1.8 kg) Ironmaster Imperial Pale Ale Kit
2 pounds (.9 kg) light dry malt extract
½ ounce (14 g) Cascade hop pellets for flavoring
½ ounce (14 g) Willamette hop plug for aroma
1 packet Yeastlab L35 California Lager yeast
¾ cup (180 ml) corn sugar for priming

1. Bring 1½ gallons (6 L) cold water to a boil. Add extracts and return to a boil. Boil 20 minutes.
2. Add Cascade flavoring hops and boil 15 minutes. Remove from heat and add Willamette hop plug. Allow to steep for 5 minutes.
3. Strain hot wort into a fermenter containing 1½ gallons (6 L) of chilled water. Rinse hops with ½ gallon (2 L) boiled water. Top off up to 5 gallons (19 L).
4. Pitch yeast when cool.
5. Ferment at ale temperatures (65–70°F, 18–21°C). Bottle when fermentation stops (2–3 weeks), using corn sugar for priming. Age 4 to 6 weeks at cellar temperature (55°F, 13°C) before drinking.

Rogue Torpedo Common Beer

INITIAL GRAVITY: 1.045–1.050
FINAL GRAVITY: 1.012–1.015

½ **pound (220 g) Vienna malt**
6.6 **pounds (3 kg) Northwest gold malt extract syrup**
2 **ounces (56 g) Northern Brewer hop pellets**
½ **ounce (14 g) Cascade hop plug for flavoring**
½ **ounce (14 g) Cascade hop plug for aroma**
1 **packet Yeastlab L35 California Lager yeast**
½ **ounce (14 g) Willamette dry hops**
¾ **cup (180 ml) corn sugar for priming**

1. Heat 1½ gallons (6 L) water to 150°F (66°C). Put the crushed grains in a grain bag and immerse in the hot water. Steep for 15 minutes in water between 150° and 170°F (66° and 77°C). Remove the grains and rinse over the brewpot with ½ gallon (2 L) boiled water. Keep the pot covered, bring to a boil, and remove from heat.
2. Add extract and Northern Brewer bittering hops. Boil for 45 minutes. Add one Cascade hop plug and boil 15 more minutes. Remove from heat and add the other Cascade hop plug. Steep for 5 minutes.
3. Strain hot wort into fermenter containing 1½ gallons (6 L) chilled water. Rinse hops with boiled water. Top off up to 5 gallons (19 L).
4. Pitch the yeast when cool.
5. Ferment at ale temperatures (60–70°F, 18–21°C). When fermentation dies down, add Willamette dry hops. Bottle when fermentation stops (2–3 weeks), using the corn sugar for priming. Age 4 to 6 weeks at cellar temperature (55°F, 13°C) before drinking.

British Ales

Bitter

Bitter is cask carbonated, dry, mildly hopped, and brewed from low gravities (and is therefore low in alcohol).

Elephant & Castle Bitter

INITIAL GRAVITY: 1.045–1.056
FINAL GRAVITY: 1.014–1.018

3.75 pounds (1.7 kg) Cooper's Bitter kit
2 pounds (.9 kg) Munton & Fison light dry malt extract
1 ounce (28 g) East Kent Goldings hop plugs for flavoring
½ ounce (14 g) Willamette hop plug for aroma
1 packet Edme ale yeast
⅔ cup (160 ml) corn sugar for priming

1. Bring 1½ gallons (6 L) cold water to a boil. Add extracts and return to a boil. Boil 15 minutes.
2. Add East Kent Goldings hops for flavoring. Boil for 15 minutes. Remove from heat and add Willamette hops for aroma. Allow to steep for 5 minutes.
3. Strain hot wort into a fermenter containing 1½ gallons (6 L) of chilled water. Rinse hops with ½ gallon (2 L) boiled water. Top off up to 5 gallons (19 L). Pitch yeast when cool.
4. Ferment at ale temperatures (65–70°F, 18–21°C). Bottle when fermentation ceases (7–10 days), using corn sugar for priming. Age 2 weeks before drinking.

Brown Ale

Brown ale is a mild, nutty, lightly hopped, and fairly low-alcohol beer.

Flying Finster Brown Ale

INITIAL GRAVITY: 1.042–1.050
FINAL GRAVITY: 1.015–1.019

4 pounds (1.8 kg) Mahogany Coast Nut Brown ale kit
2 pounds (.9 kg) Munton & Fison dark dry malt extract
½ ounce (14 g) East Kent Goldings hop plug for flavoring
1 packet Whitbread ale yeast
⅔ cup (160 ml) corn sugar for priming

1. Bring 1½ gallons (6 L) cold water to a boil. Add extracts and return to a boil. Boil 15 minutes.
2. Add East Kent Goldings flavoring hops and boil 5 minutes.
3. Strain hot wort into a fermenter containing 1½ gallons (6 L) of chilled water. Rinse hops with ½ gallon (2 L) boiled water. Top off up to 5 gallons (19 L).
4. Pitch yeast when cool.
5. Ferment at ale temperatures (65–70°F, 18–21°C). Bottle when fermentation ceases (7–10 days), using the corn sugar for priming. It should be ready to drink in 2 weeks.

Ecce Thump Brown Ale

INITIAL GRAVITY: 1.040–1.058
FINAL GRAVITY: 1.015–1.020

⅛ **pound (55 g) black patent malt**
⅓ **pound (150 g) biscuit malt**
½ **pound (220 g) British crystal malt**
6.6 **pounds (3 kg) Northwest gold malt extract syrup**
1½ **ounces (42 g) East Kent Goldings hop pellets**
½ **ounce (14 g) Fuggles hop plug for aroma**
1 to 2 **packets Edme ale yeast**
⅔ **cup (160 ml) corn sugar for priming**

1. Heat 1½ gallons (6 L) water to 150°F (66°C). Put the crushed grains in a grain bag and immerse in the hot water. Steep for 15 minutes, keeping the water temperature between 150° and 170°F. Remove the grain bag and rinse over the brewpot with ½ gallon (2 L) boiled water. Keeping the pot covered, bring to a boil, and then remove from heat.

2. Add extract and East Kent Goldings bittering hops. Return to heat and boil for 45 minutes. Remove from heat and add Fuggles hop plug. Allow to steep for 5 minutes.

3. Strain hot wort into fermenter containing 1½ gallons (6 L) chilled water. Rinse hops with boiled water. Top off up to 5 gallons (19 L).

4. Pitch the yeast when cool.

5. Ferment at ale temperatures (60–70°F, 18–21°C). Bottle when fermentation stops (1–2 weeks), using corn sugar for priming. Age 3 weeks before drinking.

Mild

Mild is light brown, very light bodied, very lightly hopped, with a malty taste—as malty as possible given the very low starting gravity. It is a good thirst-quencher at the end of the day, or as a pint at lunch.

Frantic Mild

INITIAL GRAVITY: 1.032–1.041
FINAL GRAVITY: 1.012–1.016

- 3.3 pounds (1.5 kg) Munton & Fison hopped amber malt extract syrup
- 2 pounds (.9 kg) dark dry malt extract
- 2 ounces (56 g) Fuggles hop pellets
- ½ ounce (14 g) East Kent Goldings hop plug for aroma
- 1 or 2 packets Munton & Fison Muntona ale yeast
- ⅔ cup (160 ml) corn sugar for priming

1. Bring 1½ gallons (6 L) cold water to a boil. Remove from heat and add extracts and Fuggles hop pellets. Return to heat and boil 60 minutes. Remove from heat and add East Kent Goldings hop plug. Allow to steep for 5 minutes.

2. Strain hot wort into a fermenter containing 1½ gallons (6 L) of chilled water. Rinse hops with ½ gallon (2 L) boiled water. Top off up to 5 gallons (19 L).

3. Pitch yeast when cool.

4. Ferment at ale temperatures (65–70°F, 18–21°C). Bottle when fermentation ceases (7–10 days), using corn sugar for priming. It should be ready to drink in 2 weeks.

Kew Gardens Mild

INITIAL GRAVITY: 1.036–1.043
FINAL GRAVITY: 1.014–1.018

⅓ **pound (150 g) Munich malt**
½ **pound (220 g) 60° Lovibond crystal malt**
3.3 **pounds (1.5 kg) Northwest dark malt extract syrup**
1½ **pounds (.7 kg) amber dry malt extract**
1½ **ounces (42 g) Fuggles hop pellets for bittering**
½ **ounce (14 g) Fuggles hop plug for aroma**
1 **packet Whitbread ale yeast**
⅔ **cup (160 ml) corn sugar for priming**

1. Heat 1½ gallons (6 L) water to about 150°F (66°C). Put the crushed grains in a grain bag and immerse in hot water. Allow to steep for 15 minutes, keeping the water temperature between 150°F and 170°F (66° and 77°C). Remove grain bag and rinse over brewpot with ½ gallon (2 L) boiled water. Keeping the brewpot covered, bring to a boil, and then remove from heat.
2. Add extracts and 1½ ounces (42 g) Fuggles bittering hops. Return to heat and boil 45 minutes. Remove from heat and add ½ ounce (14 g) Fuggles hop plug. Allow to steep for 5 minutes.
3. Strain hot wort into fermenter containing 1½ gallons (6 L) chilled water. Rinse hops with boiled water. Top off up to 5 gallons (19 L).
4. Pitch the yeast when cool.
5. Ferment at ale temperatures (60–70°F, 18–21°C). Bottle when fermentation stops (1–2 weeks), using corn sugar for priming. Age 3 weeks before drinking.

Pale Ale

Pale ale is an amber- to copper-colored, bitter, malty beer of medium body and alcoholic strength.

Pale Horse Pale Ale

INITIAL GRAVITY: 1.044–1.055
FINAL GRAVITY: 1.014–1.018

3.3 pounds (1.5 kg) Black Rock East India Pale Ale kit
3.3 pounds (1.5 kg) Northwest Gold malt extract syrup
½ ounce (14 g) East Kent Goldings hop plug
½ ounce (14 g) Fuggles hop plug for aroma
1 packet Whitbread ale yeast
⅔ cup (160 ml) corn sugar for priming

1. Bring 1½ gallons (6 L) cold water to a boil. Remove from heat, add extracts, and return to a boil. Boil 60 minutes.
2. Add East Kent Goldings flavoring hops and boil 15 minutes. Remove from heat and add Fuggles hop plug. Allow to steep for 5 minutes.
3. Strain hot wort into a fermenter containing 1½ gallons (6 L) of chilled water. Rinse hops with ½ gallon (2 L) boiled water. Top off up to 5 gallons (19 L).
4. Pitch yeast when cool.
5. Ferment at ale temperatures (65–70°F, 18–21°C). Bottle when fermentation ceases (7–10 days), using corn sugar for priming. It should be ready to drink in 2 weeks.

Beyond the Pale Ale

INITIAL GRAVITY: 1.044–1.055
FINAL GRAVITY: 1.014–1.018

½ **pound (220 g) 60° Lovibond British crystal malt**
¼ **pound (110 g) toasted malt**
4 **pounds (1.8 kg) Ironmaster Imperial Pale Ale kit**
2 **pounds (.9 kg) Munton & Fison amber dry malt extract**
½ **ounce (14 g) East Kent Goldings hop plug for flavoring**
½ **ounce (14 g) Willamette hop plug for aroma**
1 **packet Whitbread ale yeast**
⅔ **cup (160 ml) corn sugar for priming**

1. Heat 1½ gallons (6 L) water to about 150°F (66°C). Put the crushed grains in a grain bag and immerse in hot water. Allow to steep for 15 minutes, keeping the water temperature between 150° and 170°F (66° and 77°C). Remove grain bag and rinse over brewpot with ½ gallon (2 L) boiled water. Keeping the brewpot covered, bring to a boil, and then remove from heat.

2. Add extracts and East Kent Goldings flavoring hops. Return to heat and boil 60 minutes. Remove from heat and add Willamette hop plug. Allow to steep for 5 minutes.

3. Strain hot wort into fermenter containing 1½ gallons (6 L) chilled water. Rinse hops with boiled water. Top off up to 5 gallons (19 L).

4. Pitch the yeast when cool.

5. Ferment at ale temperatures (60–70°F, 18–21°C). Bottle when fermentation stops (2–3 weeks), using corn sugar for priming. Age 3 to 4 weeks before drinking.

Porter

Porter is a medium-bodied, moderately hopped dark ale of medium alcoholic strength.

Two Pints Off The Port Bow Porter

INITIAL GRAVITY: 1.044–1.052
FINAL GRAVITY: 1.014–1.019

4 pounds (1.8 kg) Telford's Porter Kit
3 pounds (1.4 kg) Northwest Gold Extract Syrup
1 ounce (28 g) Willamette hop plugs
1 packet Whitbread Ale yeast
½ cup (120 ml) corn sugar for priming

1. Bring 1½ gallons (6 L) cold water to a boil. Remove from heat, add extracts, and return to a boil. Boil 60 minutes.
2. Add Willamette flavoring hops and boil 5 minutes.
3. Strain hot wort into a fermenter containing 1½ gallons (6 L) of chilled water. Rinse hops with ½ gallon (2 L) boiled water. Top off up to 5 gallons (19 L).
4. Pitch yeast when cool.
5. Ferment at ale temperatures (65–70°F). Bottle when fermentation ceases (7–10 days), using corn sugar for priming. It should be ready to drink in 2 weeks.

Dunderfunk Porter

INITIAL GRAVITY: 1.040–1.049
FINAL GRAVITY: 1.010–1.015

¼ **pound (110 g) chocolate malt**
¼ **pound (110 g) roasted barley**
½ **pound (220 g) 60° Lovibond British crystal malt**
4 **pounds (1.8 kg) Mahogany Coast London Porter kit**
2½ **pounds (1.12 kg) dark dry malt extract**
1 **ounce (28 g) East Kent Goldings hop pellets**
½ **ounce (14 g) Willamette hop plug for aroma**
1 to 2 **packets Munton & Fison ale yeast**
⅔ **cup (160 ml) corn sugar for priming**

1. Heat 1½ gallons (6 L) water to about 150°F (66°C). Put the crushed grains in a grain bag and immerse in hot water. Allow to steep for 15 minutes. Keeping the water temperature between 150° and 170°F (66° and 77°C). Remove grain bag and rinse over brewpot with ½ gallon (2 L) boiled water. Keeping the brewpot covered, bring to a boil, and then remove from heat.

2. Add extracts and East Kent Goldings flavoring hops. Boil 60 minutes. Remove from heat and add Willamette hop plug. Allow to steep for 5 minutes.

3. Strain hot wort into fermenter containing 1½ gallons (6 L) chilled water. Rinse hops with boiled water. Top off up to 5 gallons (19 L).

4. Pitch the yeast when cool.

5. Ferment at ale temperatures (60–70°F, 18–21°C). Bottle when fermentation stops (2–3 weeks), using corn sugar for priming. Age 3 to 4 weeks before drinking.

Stout

Stout is a black, bitter, and complex brew. Variations include dry, sweet, imperial, and oatmeal stout. Stouts are usually fairly low in alcohol, with no hop flavor or aroma but plenty of bitterness.

Finn McCool's Irish Stout

INITIAL GRAVITY: 1.045–1.064
FINAL GRAVITY: 1.012–1.016

½ pound (220 g) 60° Lovibond British crystal malt
½ pound (220 g) roasted barley
4 pounds (1.8 kg) Telford's Gaelic Stout Kit
3 pounds (1.4 kg) Northwest dark malt extract syrup
1 ounce (28 g) Eroica hop pellets
1 packet Whitbread ale yeast
⅔ cup (160 ml) corn sugar for priming

1. Heat 1½ gallons (6 L) water to about 150°F (66°C). Put the crushed grains in a grain bag and immerse in hot water. Allow to steep for 15 minutes, keeping the water temperature between 150° and 170°F (66° and 77°C). Remove grain bag and rinse over brewpot with ½ gallon (2 L) boiled water. Keeping the brewpot covered, bring to a boil, and then remove from heat.
2. Add extracts and Eroica hops. Boil 60 minutes.
3. Strain hot wort into fermenter containing 1½ gallons (6 L) chilled water. Rinse hops with boiled water. Top off up to 5 gallons (19 L).
4. Pitch the yeast when cool.
5. Ferment at ale temperatures (60–70°F 18–21°C). Bottle when fermentation stops (2–3 weeks), using corn sugar for priming. Age 3 to 4 weeks before drinking.

Susan's Sweet Stout

INITIAL GRAVITY: 1.050–1.055
FINAL GRAVITY: 1.016–1.019

3.75 pounds (1.75 kg) Black Rock Miner's Stout
2 pounds (.9 kg) Munton & Fison dark dry malt
    extract
½ pound (220 g) dry wheat extract
1 ounce (28 g) Northern Brewer bittering hops
¼ pound (110 g) lactose
1 to 2 packets Munton & Fison ale yeast
½ cup (120 ml) corn sugar or 1 cup (240 ml) dry
    malt extract for priming

1. Bring 1½ gallons (6 L) cold water to a boil. Remove
from heat, add extracts, and return to a boil.
2. Add Northern Brewer bittering hops. Boil 60 minutes.
Add lactose for the final 15 minutes of boil.
3. Strain hot wort into a fermenter containing 1½ gallons
(6 L) chilled water. Top off up to 5 gallons (19 L).
4. Pitch yeast when cool.
5. Ferment at ale temperatures (60–70°F, 18–21°C).
Bottle when fermentation stops (2–3 weeks), using
corn sugar or malt extract for primage. Age 3 weeks
before drinking.

German Wheat Beers

Weizenbier

Weizen, or weiss, is a copper-colored, lightly hopped Bavarian wheat beer. Weizenbiers are spicy, cloudy, and slightly sour from the wheat and assertive yeast used to brew them.

Stands to Weizen

INITIAL GRAVITY: 1.045–1.050
FINAL GRAVITY: 1.014–1.016

3.3 pounds (1.5 kg) Northwest Weizen syrup
2 pounds (.9 kg) Munton & Fison dry wheat malt
½ ounce (14 g) Hallertau hop plug
1 packet Yeastlab W51 Bavarian Weizen yeast
⅞ cup (210 ml) corn sugar for priming

1. Bring 1½ gallons (6 L) cold water to a boil. Remove from heat, add extracts, and return to a boil.
2. Add Hallertau bittering hops. Boil 60 minutes.
3. Strain hot wort into a fermenter containing 1½ gallons (6 L) chilled water. Top off up to 5 gallons (19 L). Pitch yeast when cool.
4. Ferment at ale temperatures (60–70°F, 18–21°C). Bottle when fermentation stops (1–2 weeks), using corn sugar for priming. Age 3 weeks before drinking.

There's Always a Reason to Pour More Weizen

INITIAL GRAVITY: 1.059–1.063
FINAL GRAVITY: 1.016–1.019

½ pound (220 g) Special Roast malt
4 pounds (1.8 kg) Edme Superbrew Weizen kit
3.3 pounds (1.5 kg) Northwest Weizen syrup
½ ounce (14 g) Tettnang hop plug for bittering
1 packet Yeastlab W51 Bavarian Weissen yeast
⅞ cup (210 ml) corn sugar for priming

1. Heat 1½ gallons (6 L) water to about 150°F (66°C). Put the crushed grains in a grain bag and immerse in hot water. Allow to steep for 15 minutes, keeping the water temperature between 150° and 170°F (66° and 77°C). Remove grain bag and rinse over the brewpot with ½ gallon (2 L) boiled water. Keeping the brewpot covered, bring to a boil, and then remove from heat.
2. Add extracts and return to a boil. Add Tettnang hop plug. Boil 60 minutes.
3. Strain hot wort into a fermenter containing 1½ gallons (6 L) chilled water. Rinse hops with boiled water. Top off up to 5 gallons (19 L).
4. Pitch yeast when cool.
5. Ferment at ale temperatures (60–70°F, 18–21°C). Bottle when fermentation ceases (1–2 weeks), using corn sugar for priming. Age 3 weeks before drinking.

German Lagers

Bock

Bock is a sweet, malty, full-bodied lager. There are many versions, including the more powerful Dopplebock.

Headlock Bock

INITIAL GRAVITY: 1.060–1.065
FINAL GRAVITY: 1.011–1.014

⅛ **pound (55 g) Munich malt**
⅛ **pound (55 g) 90° Lovibond German crystal malt**
6 **pounds (2.7 kg) Northwest dark malt extract syrup**
2 **ounces (56 g) Tettnang hop pellets for bittering**
1 **packet European Lager yeast**
½ **cup (120 ml) corn sugar for priming**

1. Heat 1½ gallons (6 L) water to 150°F (66°C). Put crushed grains in a grain bag and immerse in hot water. Steep for 15 minutes in water between 150° and 170°F (66° and 77°C). Remove grain bag and rinse over brewpot with ½ gallon (2 L) boiled water. Keep the brewpot covered, bring to a boil, and then turn the heat off.
2. Add extracts and return to a boil. Add Tettnang hop pellets. Boil 60 minutes.
3. Strain hot wort into a fermenter containing 1½ gallons (6 L) chilled water. Rinse hops with boiled water. Top off up to 5 gallons (19 L).
4. Pitch yeast when cool.
5. Ferment at lager temperature (40–50°F, 4–10°C). Bottle when fermentation stops (6–8 weeks), using corn sugar for priming. Age 6 to 8 weeks at lager temperature before drinking.

Dopplebock

Dopplebock is a maltier, stronger version of bock, brewed from a higher original gravity than bock. It is a heavy beverage with a strong alcohol character.

Monitor Dopplebock

INITIAL GRAVITY: 1.074–1.080
FINAL GRAVITY: 1.015–1.019

7.5 pounds (3.4 kg) Black Rock Bock kit
2 pounds (1.4 kg) Dutch light dry malt extract
1 ounce (28 g) Tettnang hop pellets
1 packet European lager yeast
½ cup (120 ml) corn sugar for priming

1. Bring 1½ gallons (6 L) cold water to a boil. Remove from heat, add extracts, and return to a boil. Add Tettnang hop pellets and boil 60 minutes.
2. Strain hot wort into a fermenter containing 1½ gallons (6 L) chilled water. Top off up to 5 gallons (19 L).
3. Pitch yeast when cool.
4. Ferment at lager temperature (40–50°F, 4–10°C). Bottle when fermentation stops (6–8 weeks), using corn sugar for priming. Age 1 to 4 months at lager temperature before drinking.

German Pilsner

German Pilsner is light-bodied, pale, dry, and assertively hopped.

Graf Zeppelin Pils

INITIAL GRAVITY: 1.040–1.045
FINAL GRAVITY: 1.010–1.015

3.3 pounds (1.5 kg) Brewferm Pilsner kit
2 pounds (.9 kg) Dutch extra light malt extract
1 ounce (28 g) Hallertau hop plugs for flavoring
½ ounce (14 g) Saaz hop plug for aroma
1 packet Yeastlab dry European lager yeast
¾ cup (180 ml) corn sugar for priming

1. Bring 1½ gallons (6 L) cold water to a boil. Remove from heat, add extracts and return to a boil. Boil 60 minutes.
2. Add Hallertau hops and boil 15 minutes. Remove from heat, add Saaz hop plug, and allow to steep for 5 minutes.
3. Strain hot wort into a fermenter containing 1½ gallons (6 L) chilled water. Top off up to 5 gallons (19 L).
4. Pitch yeast when cool.
5. Ferment at lager temperature (40–50°F, 4–10°C). Bottle when fermentation stops (6–8 weeks), using corn sugar for priming. Age 1 to 4 months at lager temperature before drinking.

Tiny Ragged Pils

INITIAL GRAVITY: 1.048–1.052
FINAL GRAVITY: 1.014–1.018

- ½ **pound (220 g) Vienna malt**
- 3.3 **pounds (1.5 kg) Bierkeller light unhopped malt extract syrup**
- 2 **pounds (.9 kg) Dutch extra light malt extract**
- 1½ **ounces (42 g) Hallertau hop pellets**
- ½ **ounce (14 g) Tettnang hop plug for flavoring**
- ½ **ounce (14 g) Hallertau hop plug for aroma**
- 1 **packet Yeastlab dry European lager yeast**
- ¾ **cup (180 ml) corn sugar for priming**

1. Heat 1½ gallons (6 L) water to about 150°F (66°C). Put the crushed grains in a grain bag and immerse in hot water. Allow to steep for 15 minutes, keeping the water temperature between 150° and 170°F (66°and 77°C). Remove grain bag and rinse over brewpot with ½ gallon (2 L) boiled water. Keeping the brewpot covered, bring to a boil, and then remove from heat.

2. Add 1½ ounces (42 g) Hallertau hops and boil 60 minutes. Add Tettnang hop plug for flavoring in the last 15 minutes of boil. Add Hallertau hop plug for aroma, and allow to steep for 5 minutes.

3. Strain hot wort into a fermenter containing 1½ gallons (6 L) chilled water. Top off up to 5 gallons (19 L).

4. Pitch yeast when cool.

5. Ferment at lager temperature (40–50°F, 4–10°C). Bottle when fermentation stops (6–8 weeks), using corn sugar for priming. Age 1 to 4 months at lager temperature before drinking.

Belgian Ales

Dubbel

Dubbel and Tripel are two of the Belgian Trappist ales produced by monks living in this beer-intensive region.

Bishop's Ruin Dubbel

INITIAL GRAVITY: 1.070–1.076
FINAL GRAVITY: 1.014–1.017

- 1 teaspoon Irish moss
- 3.3 pounds (1.5 kg) Brewferm Abbey
- 4 pounds (1.8 kg) Alexander's plain light malt extract syrup
- ½ pound (220 g) brown sugar
- 1 ounce (28 g) Styrian Goldings Hop plugs
- 1 ounce (28 g) Saaz hop plugs for aroma
- 1 packet Yeastlab A08 Trappist ale yeast
- ¾ cup (180 ml) corn sugar for priming

1. Bring 1½ gallons (6 L) cold water to a boil. Remove from heat and add extracts, brown sugar, and Irish moss. Return to heat and boil 60 minutes.
2. Add Styrian Goldings hop plugs in the last 10 minutes of boil. Remove from heat, add Saaz hop plugs, and allow to steep 5 minutes.
3. Strain hot wort into fermenter containing 1½ gallons (6 L) chilled water. Rinse hops with boiled water. Top off up to 5 gallons (19 L).
4. Pitch yeast when cool.
5. Ferment at ale temperatures (60–70 °F, 18–21 °C). Bottle when fermentation ceases (3–6 weeks), using corn sugar for priming. Age 6 weeks before drinking.

Tripel

Tripel is fruity, estery, and strongly alcoholic. It ages well and continues to develop in the bottle.

Rose Window Tripel

INITIAL GRAVITY: 1.076–1.080
FINAL GRAVITY: 1.016–1.018

½ **pound (220 g) British crystal malt**
½ **pound (220 g) Cara Munich malt**
¼ **pound (110 g) Cara Vienna malt**
6 **pounds (2.7 kg) Northwest Gold malt extract syrup**
3 **pounds honey (1.4 kg)**
1 **ounce (28 g) Styrian Goldings hop pellets**
½ **ounce (14 g) Saaz dry hops**
1 **packet Yeastlab A08 Trappist ale yeast**
¾ **cup (180 ml) corn sugar for priming**

1. Heat 1½ gallons (6 L) water to about 150°F (66°C). Put the crushed grains in a grain bag and immerse in hot water. Steep for 15 minutes in water between 150° and 170° F (66° and 77°C). Remove grain bag and rinse over brewpot with ½ gallon (2 L) boiled water. Keep the brewpot covered, bring to a boil, and remove from heat.
2. Add extract syrup, honey, and Styrian Goldings hop pellets. Boil for 45 minutes.
3. Strain hot wort into a fermenter containing 1½ gallons (6 L) chilled water. Top off up to 5 gallons (19 L).
4. Pitch yeast when cool.
5. Ferment at ale temperatures (60–70°F, 18–21°C). When fermentation begins to die down, add Saaz dry hops to fermenter. Bottle when fermentation ceases (3–6 weeks), using corn sugar for priming. Age 6 to 8 weeks before drinking.

Duvel

Duvel (Belgian for "devil") could fairly be described as a "stealth" ale; it looks, smells, and tastes like a pilsner, but it's much stronger. Imbibe with care.

Beelzebub Duvel

INITIAL GRAVITY: 1.080–1.084
FINAL GRAVITY: 1.012–1.016

½ **pound (220 g) Vienna malt**
6.6 **pounds (3 kg) Breferm Diabolo kit (2 cans)**
2 **pounds (.9 kg) orange blossom honey**
½ **ounce (14 g) Saaz hop plug**
1 **packet Yeastlab A08 Trappist ale yeast**
⅔ **cup (160 ml) corn sugar for priming**

1. Heat 1½ gallons (6 L) water to about 150°F (66°C). Put the crushed grains in a grain bag and immerse in hot water. Allow to steep for 15 minutes, keeping the water temperature between 150° and 170°F (66° and 77°C). Remove grain bag and rinse over brewpot with ½ gallon (2 L) boiled water. Keeping the brewpot covered, bring to a boil, and then remove from heat.
2. Add extract and honey and boil 60 minutes. Remove from heat and add Saaz hop plug. Allow to steep 5 minutes.
3. Strain hot wort into a fermenter containing 1½ gallons (6 L) chilled water. Top off up to 5 gallons (19 L).
4. Pitch yeast when cool.
5. Ferment at ale temperatures (60–70°F, 18–21°C). Bottle when fermentation ceases (3–6 weeks), using corn sugar for priming. Age 6 weeks before drinking.

Glossary

Ale: Style of beer produced by top-fermenting yeast strains at relatively warm temperatures. Includes bitter, stout, porter, India Pale, and others.

Alpha acids: The acids that form the main bittering agents in hops.

Barley: A cereal grain, the seeds of which (barleycorns) are used in making beer. There are different varieties, 2-row and 6-row, which have different characteristics.

Carboy: A clear plastic or glass bottle that can be used as a fermenting vessel.

Cold break: The stage during the cooling of hot wort when proteins precipitate as suspended particles.

Conditioning: The stage during beer aging when carbonation develops.

Esters: Organic compounds that often have strong, fruity aromas.

Fermentation: The stage of the yeast's life cycle during which it eats and produces alcohol, carbon dioxide, and some flavors of beer.

Fermentation lock: A device that vents carbon dioxide from a vessel while keeping air out, preventing contamination.

Fining agent: An ingredient used to clarify beer, such as gelatin, Irish moss, and isinglass.

Finishing hops: Hops added after the boil that contribute delicate aromas to the beer.

Hydrometer: A graduated glass instrument used to measure the specific gravity of liquids such as unfermented wort and finished beer.

Kraeusen: The large head of foam that forms on the surface of the wort during the early stages of fermentation.

Isomerization: The process in which the arrangement—but not the number or kind—of atoms in a compound are altered by heating or other means. During boiling, alpha acids in hops are isomerized and these isomers (iso-alpha acids) bitter the finished beer.

Lager: Style of beer produced by bottom-fermenting yeasts at low temperatures. Originated in Germany. Includes maerzens, pilsners, bocks, and Oktoberfests, among others.

Malt: Cereal grain (generally barley, but not always) that has been partially germinated, dried, or possibly roasted to produce different brewing characteristics.

Malt extract: Concentrated wort in syrup or powder form. Can be hopped or unhopped.

Mashing: The process of extracting sweet liquor from malted grains by means of temperature-controlled steeping.

Pitching: Adding yeast to wort to begin the fermentation process.

Primary fermentation: The very active first phase of fermentation that proceeds from the time of pitching until the kraeusen drops.

Primary fermenter: Vessel in which primary fermentation takes place. Can be either a plastic bucket or a carboy.

Priming: The process of adding sugar or malt extract to beer at bottling time to induce carbonation.

Racking: The process of siphoning unfinished homebrew from the primary fermentation vessel to the secondary fermentation vessel or bottling bucket.

Secondary fermentation: The less active, later stage of fermentation that proceeds from the time the kraeusen subsides until the yeast drops out of the solution.

Secondary fermenter: Vessel in which secondary fermentation takes place. Can be a carboy, plastic bucket, or keg.

Sparging: The process of rinsing residual sugars from mashed grains with boiled water.

Specific gravity: The weight of a liquid compared with an equal amount of pure water.

Wort: The unfermented solution of malt sugars, proteins, and other substances. Once fermentation is complete, it is called "beer."

Yeast: Microscopic organisms that produce the alcohol, carbon dioxide, and some of the flavors of beer through their life cycle.

Amounts and Conversions

Liquid Measures

1 US gallon = 3.785 liters
1 US gallon = .833 Imperial gallons
1 Imperial gallon = 1.2 US gallons
1 Imperial pint = 20 ounces
1 US pint = 2 cups = 473 milliliters

Dry Measures

¼	pound	= 113 grams
½	pound	= 227 grams
¾	pound	= 340 grams
1	pound	= 454 grams
1½	pounds	= 680 grams
1¾	pounds	= 794 grams
2	pounds	= 907 grams
3.3	pounds	= 1.5 kilograms
3.75	pounds	= 1.7 kilograms

Temperature

Degrees Celsius = $\frac{5}{9}$ (F minus 32)
Degrees Fahrenheit = ($\frac{9}{5}$ x C) + 32

Appendix B

How to Use the Hydrometer

The hydrometer is a graduated glass instrument that measures the density or specific gravity of liquids. It is ordinarily used twice in basic brewing: first to test the specific gravity of the unfermented wort, and second to find the gravity of the finished beer. The initial reading is taken after the wort has been topped off up to 5 gallons but before the yeast is pitched, and it gives the brewer an idea of the amount of fermentables in the wort (original gravity). The second reading is used to confirm that fermentation is complete (final gravity). If your recipe is provided with initial and finished gravity readings and you have followed it exactly, then your readings should fall within the range given. Yeast converts sugars in the fermentables into alcohol and CO_2, so your final reading will always be less than your initial reading. A hydrometer reading that is higher than it ought to be may indicate that fermentation is not complete.

To take a reading, fill the plastic hydrometer container case with wort to about ½ inch from the top. Place the hydrometer in the wort and gently spin it with your fingers to remove air bubbles. Find where the liquid crosses the scale in the neck of the hydrometer. Write down this figure. When reading a hydrometer, you should sight directly across the top of the liquid to get a true reading.

The density of pure water is considered to be 1.000 at 59°F (15°C). You will probably be measuring liquids that are much warmer, in the 70° to 90°F range, so you need to make an adjustment or correction of an additional .001 for every 10° greater than 59°F. Thus, if your wort measures 1.035 at 90°F, then you would add .003 to 1.035 for an initial gravity reading of 1.038.

When you feel that fermentation
is complete, take another reading. If
it falls within the range given in your
recipe, then you can safely bottle
your beer. If not, wait a week and take
another reading. If your reading falls
within the given range, proceed with
bottling. If it is unchanged, or re-
mains high, then your fermentation
may still be unfinished.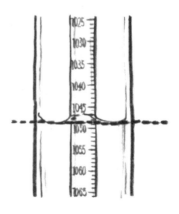

Assuming that your beer is finished, you can now determine how much alcohol is in it. To use your hydrometer's
potential alcohol scale, you simply subtract the final reading
on the scale from the initial reading. You can also subtract
the final gravity from the initial gravity, and multiply by 105
to get percent alcohol by weight (abw). The alcohol content
of beer varies from 3 percent in low-alcohol brews to 10 or
11 percent in a serious brew. Most beers will typically be
close to 5 percent alcohol.

The hydrometer that comes with the equipment kit is likely
to be very delicate and requires careful handling. The first one
we had broke from temperature stress while being sanitized.
Some of the more expensive models are more durable. Because
the hydrometer never touches the potential beer, it does not
need to be sanitized, but it should be kept clean. The plastic
sampling tube will need to be sanitized, unless you are using a
wine thief or turkey baster to fill it (in which case, you must
sanitize either of them).

NOTE: Pour the wort sample down the sink. If you return it to
the fermenter, you could contaminate your beer.

Appendix C

Sources

Locate your nearest homebrewing supply shop by checking the local Yellow Pages, which should have a listing under "Brewing Supplies," "Winemaking Supplies," or "Beer—Homebrewing Supplies." Even if they do not carry what you need, they may be able to special-order it for you.

Another source of good information is your local homebrewing club. Most metropolitan areas now have one or more. These experienced homebrewers will be happy to share their experiences. One way to find out about a local club is through your local homebrew supply shop. In addition, the American Homebrewers Association has a list of all the clubs in the country that are registered with it, and will gladly tell you if there is a registered club in your area. Contact American Homebrewers Association, PO Box 1679, Boulder, CO 80306; 303/447-0816.

Homebrewing magazines also have a lot to offer the new brewer. Along with lots of information, the magazines have many advertisements for mail-order dealers and manufacturers of special equipment. Start by subscribing to *Zymurgy,* the magazine of the American Homebrewers Association (at the address given above). *Brew Your Own: The How-To Homebrew Beer Magazine* is another great monthly. Subscribe by writing to them at PO Box 1504, Martinez, CA 94553-9932. Or fax them at 510/372-8582.

Brewing Techniques is also an excellent magazine, covering the advanced, more technical side of homebrewing. Subscribe by calling 800/427-2993, or write to them at PO Box 3222, Eugene, OR 97403, or by e-mail: btcirc@aol.com. *Brewing Techniques* also features ads for equipment and ingredient suppliers.

Another source of information is the beer and wine forums now available on most of the major online computer services. These forums do not carry ads, of course, but a specific question will usually draw a number of replies from experienced people. Especially for those who live in sparsely populated areas, the online services can be an excellent way to connect with other homebrewers.

Recommended Reading

Anderson, Mark R. "Enhance Your Beer-Drinking Pleasure with the Proper Glass." *Zymurgy* 18, no. 1 (1995): 58.

Baker, Patrick. *The New Brewer's Handbook.* Westport, MA: Crosby & Baker Books, 1979, 1995.

Burch, Byron. *Brewing Quality Beers.* San Rafael, CA: Joby Books, 1986, 1991.

Eames, Alan D. *Secret Life of Beer: Legends, Lore & Little-Known Facts.* Pownal, VT: Storey Publishing, 1995.

Eckhardt, Fred. *The Essentials of Beer Style.* Portland, OR: Fred Eckhardt Communications, 1989.

Fisher, Joe, and Dennis Fisher. *Great Beer from Kits.* Pownal, VT: Storey Publishing, 1996.

Jackson, Michael. *Michael Jackson's Beer Companion.* Philadelphia, PA: Running Press, 1993.

Lutzen, Karl F., and Mark Stevens. *Brew Ware: How to Find, Adapt & Build Homebrewing Equipment.* Pownal, VT: Storey Publishing, 1996.

———. *Homebrew Favorites.* Pownal, VT: Storey Publishing, 1994.

Mares, William. *Making Beer.* New York: Knopf, 1984, 1994.

Miller, Dave. *Brewing the World's Great Beers: A Step-by-Step Guide.* Pownal, VT: Storey Publishing, 1992.

———. *The Complete Handbook of Home Brewing.* Pownal, VT: Storey Publishing, 1988.

———. *Dave Miller's Homebrewing Guide: Everything you need to know to make great-tasting beer.* Pownal, VT: Storey Publishing, 1995.

Mosher, Randy. *The Brewer's Companion.* Seattle, WA: Alephenalia Publications, 1994.

Papazian, Charlie. *The New Complete Joy of Home Brewing.* New York: Avon Books, 1984, 1991.

Wearne, Jim. *Basic Homebrewing.* Pownal, VT: A Storey Publishing Bulletin, A-144, 1995.

Weisberg, David. *50 Great Homebrewing Tips.* Peterborough, NH: Lampman Brewing Publications, 1994.

Weix, Patrick. "Become *Saccharomyces* Savvy." *Zymurgy* 17, no. 2 (1994): 44.

Index

Note: Page numbers in *italics* indicate illustrations.

Adjuncts, 23
Aging beer, 22
Airlock (fermentation lock), 8,
    8, 15, *15*, 41, *41*, 50
Ales
    Belgian, 75–77
    British, 58–68
    lagers compared to, 52
Alpha acids, 29, 37

Beelzebub Duvel, 77
Belgian ales
    dubbel, 75
    duvel, 77
    tripel, 76
Beyond the Pale Ale, 64
Bishop's Ruin Dubbel, 75
Bitter, 58
Blow-by system, 49, *49*
Bock, 71
Boil, full, 11
Bottle caps, 16, *16*, 18, 22,
    22, 54
Bottles, 17, *17*, 18, *18*, 22,
    22, 52
Bottle washer, 42, *42*
Bottling, steps in, 18–*22*, *18–22*

Bottling bucket, 16, *16*, 18, 19,
    19, 21, *21*
Brewpot, 8, *8*, 11–12, *11*, *12*
British ales
    bitter, 58
    brown, 59–60
    mild, 61–62
    pale, 63–64
    porter, 65–66
    stout, 67–68
Brown ale, 59–60
Brush, bottle/carboy, 42, *42*

California Common, 56–57
Capper, 16, *16*, 18, 22, *22*
Carboy, 12, 13, *13*, 42, *42*
    blow-by system and, 49, *49*
    cleaning, 51
    emptying, 50–51
    handling tips, 51, *51*
    jacket for, 50
Cleansers/sanitizers, 43
Cold break, 10
Cold-water bath, 14, *14*
Color, selecting malt extracts
    for, 35–36
Corn sugar, 17, 20

Demologos Common Beer, 56
Dopplebock, 72
Dubbel, 75
Dunderfunk Porter, 66
Duvel, 77

Ecce Thump Brown Ale, 60
Elephant & Castle Bitter, 58
Equipment, 8–9, *8, 9,*, 16–17, *16, 17,* 41–46, *41–46*
Extracts, malt. *See* Malt extracts.

Fermentables, estimating, 39
Fermentation, primary and secondary, 48, *48*
Fermentation lock (airlock), 8, *8,* 15, *15,* 41, *41,* 50
Fermenting bucket, 8, *8,* 15, *15*
Filler wand, 17, *17,* 18
Finings, 32, 34
Finn McCool's Irish Stout, 67
Flying Finster Brown Ale, 59
Frantic Mild, 61
Funnel, 43, *43*

Gelatin, unflavored, 17, 20, 34
German lagers, 71–74
German pilsner, 73
German wheat beers, 69–70
Glasses, beer, 53
Graf Zeppelin Pils, 73
Grain mill, 44, *44*
Grains, malt. *See* Malt grains.
Gravity. *See* Specific gravity.

Headlock Bock, 71
Hop bag, 44, *44*
Hops, 28–29, *28*
    bittering, 29
    finishing, 29
    flavoring, 29

selecting, 37
    varieties of, 29–30
Hydrometer/hydrometer tube, 8, *8,* 13, *13,* 15
    how to use, 81–82

Ingredients, 23
    finings, 32, 34
    hops, 28–30, *28*
    malt extracts, 24–25
    malt grains, 25–28, *27, 28*
    for priming, 17, 20
    selecting, *see* Recipe formulation.
    yeast, 31–33, *31, 32*
Irish moss, 34

Kettles, 45, 45
Kew Gardens Mild, 62
Kraeusen, 49

Labels, 53
Lagers
    ales compared to, 52
    German, 71–74
Lovibond, 24

Malt extracts, 5–6
    adding dry malt extract, 47
    bottling equipment, list of, 16–17, *16, 17*
    bottling steps, 18–22, *18–22*
    brewing equipment, list of, 8–9, *8, 9*
    brewing steps, 6, 10–15, *10–15*
    can kits, 25
    dry, 25
    priming, 15, 17, 20
    recipe, brewing your first, 7
    sanitizing, 9, 10, 18, *18*

selecting, 35–36
syrup, 24
yeast, adding, 14
Malt grains, 25
   adding them to beer, 27
   bags and how to use them,
      27–28, *27, 28*
   color, selecting malt extracts
      by, 35–36
   varieties of, 26
Measurements, conversions
   of, 80
Mild, 61–62
Monitor Dopplebock, 72

Notebook, 45, *45*

Pale ale, 63–64
Pale Horse Pale Ale, 63
Pilsner, German, 73
Porter, 65–66
Priming, 15
   ingredients for, 17, 20

Racking, 48, *48*
Recipe formulation, 34, 39–40
   hops, selecting, 37
   malt extracts, selecting,
      35–36
   style, selecting, 35, 40
   water, selecting and adjust-
      ing, 38–39
   yeast, selecting, 38
Recipes. *See also* Styles.
   Beelzebub Duvel, 77
   Beyond the Pale Ale, 64
   Bishop's Ruin Dubbel, 75
   Demologos Common Beer, 56
   Dunderfunk Porter, 66
   Ecce Thump Brown Ale, 60

Elephant & Castle Bitter, 58
Finn McCool's Irish Stout, 67
Flying Finster Brown Ale, 59
Frantic Mild, 61
Graf Zeppelin Pils, 73
Headlock Bock, 71
Kew Gardens Mild, 62
Monitor Dopplebock, 72
Pale Horse Pale Ale, 63
Redemption Bitter, 7
Rogue Torpedo Common
   Beer, 57
Rose Window Tripel, 76
Stands to Weizen, 69
Susan's Sweet Stout, 68
There's Always a Reason to
   Pour More Weizen, 70
Tiny Ragged Pils, 74
Two Pints Off the Port Bow
   Porter, 65
Redemption Bitter, 7
Rogue Torpedo Common
   Beer, 57
Rolling pin, using to crush
   grain, 44, *44*
Rose Window Tripel, 76

Sanitizing, 9, 10, 18, *18*
   cleansers/sanitizers for, 43
Saucepans, 17, *17*
Scale, 45, *45*
Serving tips, 53, 54
Siphon tubing, 16, *16,* 19, *19,*
   21, *21,* 49, *49*
Specific gravity
   measuring, 13, 15
   selecting malt extracts by,
      35–36
Spoon, stirring, 8, *8,* 16, *16,*
Stands to Weizen, 69

Stopper, 46
Storing beer, 22
Stout, 67–68
Strainer, 46, *46*
Styles. *See also* Recipes.
  ales and lagers compared, 52
  Belgian ales, 75–77
  bitter, 58
  bock, 71
  British ales, 58–68
  brown ale, 59–60
  California Common, 56–57
  dopplebock, 72
  dubbel, 75
  duvel, 77
  German lagers, 71–74
  German pilsner, 73
  German wheat beers, 69–70
  introduction to, 55
  mild, 61–62
  pale ale, 63–64
  porter, 65–66
  selecting, 35, 40
  stout, 67–68
  tripel, 76
  weizenbier, 69–70
Sugar, corn, 17, 20
Susan's Sweet Stout, 68

Thermometer, 9, *9*
There's Always a Reason to
    Pour More Weizen, 70
Timer, 9, *9, 18*
Tiny Ragged Pils, 74
Tripel, 76
Tubing, siphon, 16, *16,* 18, 19,
    19, 21, *21,* 49, *49*
Two Pints Off the Port Bow
    Porter, 65

Water, selecting and adjust
    ing, 38–39
Weizenbier, 69–70
Wheat beers, German, 69–70
Wort chiller, 46, *46*
  alternative to, 48, *48*

Yeast
  adding, *14*
  bottom-fermenting, 31
  dried, 31–33, *31*
  liquid, 32, 33
  packs of, 32, *32*
  selecting, 38
  top-fermenting, 31
  varieties of, 33

Other Storey Titles You Will Enjoy

The Beer Directory: An International Guide, by Heather Wood. A world-wide beer-lovers' directory with more than 4500 listings of large and small breweries, places to enjoy good beer such as pubs and restaurants, places of historical "beer" interest, festivals, celebrations, magazines and publications, organizations, and even beer-oriented travel groups and agencies. 224 pages. Paperback. US $12.95 / CAN $17.95. Order #903-6.

The Beer Enthusiast's Guide: Tasting & Judging Brews from Around the World, by Gregg Smith. A guidebook to recognizing and appreciating the world's great beers. Covers brewing history, evaluating techniques, ingredients, and beer styles and characteristics. Also includes a study guide for the Beer Judge Certification Program. 144 pages. Paperback. US $12.95 / CAN $17.95. Order #838-2.

Better Beer & How to Brew It, by M.R. Reese. With this illustrated step-by-step guide, beginners can learn how easy and inexpensive it is to brew beer at home. Covers everything the beginner needs to brew, from choosing the equipment and ingredients, to preparing, fermenting, and aging, to bottling and serving. Includes 19 easy-to-brew recipes for beer and ale. 128 pages. Paperback. US $9.95 / CAN $13.95. Order #257-0.

Country Wines: Making and Using Wines from Herbs, Fruits, Flowers & More, by Pattie Vargas and Rich Gulling. Comprehensive information on how to make delicious wines from fruits and berries, flowers, and herbs. 176 pages. Paperback. US $12.95 / CAN $17.95. Order #749-1.

From Vines to Wines: The Complete Guide to Growing Grapes and Making Your Own Wine, by Jeff Cox. Takes the home winemaker through the entire process, from evaluating the site and choosing the best grape species to vineyard care, bottling, supplies, and troubleshooting. 288 pages. Paperback. US $14.95 / CAN $20.95. Order #528-6.

Great Beer from Kits, by Joe Fisher and Dennis Fisher. Anticipates the questions and concerns of the hundreds of novice homebrewers who decide to make beer from kits. A complete reference that warns of the pitfalls inherent in the "how-to brochures" that accompany such kits and explains basic brewing techniques and equipment, with step-by-step directions for all phases. 176 pages. Paperback. US $12.95 / CAN $17.95. Order #911-7.

Sweet and Hard Cider: Making It, Using It & Enjoying It, by Annie Proulx and Lew Nichols. A comprehensive guide to every aspect of cider making. Topics include the cidering process, equipment, apple varieties, recipes, and more. 192 pages. Paperback. US $12.95 /CAN $17.95. Order #352-6.

These books and other Storey books are available from your bookstore, farm store, garden center, or directly from Storey Publishing, Schoolhouse Road, Pownal, VT 05261, or by calling 1-800-441-5700.